ELON K. TALMIE

Crown Jewels

Revelations from the Royal Treasury of the Kingdom of God

Elon K. Talmie
St. Mary
Jamaica
West Indies
Tel: 876-282-1108
Email: ambassadortalmie@yahoo.com

ISBN: 978 976 96086 0 3

DEDICATION

This book is dedicated firstly to my beautiful, lovely wife and partner in ministry, Stacey Talmie, who, through the best of times and the worst of times, has been and continues to be a source of inspiration and motivation.

Secondly, to my three wonderful and amazing children: Brianna, Annice and Ethan.

Thirdly, to the citizens of the Kingdom of God who are passionate about the Word of God and who possess a heart to see His Kingdom come and His will being done in earth just as it is in Heaven.

TABLE OF CONTENTS

Acknowledgements   6

Introduction   7

King of Kings of Kings   12

His Train Fills the Temple   28

There's a Lion in Your Praise   42

Precious Cargo on Board   58

Behold I Give unto You Power   76

The Power of Agreement   96

Conditioning Your Condition   120

Poetic Declaration   142

About Kabowd Ministries   145

ACKNOWLEDGEMENTS

I wish to express sincere gratitude to my family for their patience and understanding as I took time to focus on the completion of this book. Stacey, my wife, my other half, this perhaps would not have been completed, had it not been for you and the spirit in you; and also my children: Brianna, Annice and Ethan - the divine blessings of God in my life.

To my parents who established a godly environment in our home while growing up: my mother, Maureen Talmie, who woke us up at 5 o'clock almost every morning for devotions and my father, Hubert Talmie, whose love for and understanding of the Word of God impacted greatly on my life and ministry.

Thanks to Ralph Somers, Founder and Senior Pastor of Kingdom of Heaven Embassy Ministries (KHEM), for your kind support and selfless contribution toward the completion of this work.

Also to the ministers and ministries who have encouraged, motivated, mentored or interceded for us - my heartfelt gratitude to you all.

INTRODUCTION

Some of the greatest hymns ever penned came from the lips of the patriarchs of the Old Testament as they belted out adoration to God in verbal expressions that could only flow from the heart of true worshippers. Exodus chapter fifteen gives us one of these great lyrical compositions, performed by Moses, accompanied by a mass choir of over two million voices strong. This impromptu choral was inspired by the mighty deliverance that God wrought on their behalf when He parted the Red Sea, allowing the Israelites, His chosen people, to pass through on dry ground. Just a matter of hours before, they were huddled together on the other side, crying to God and murmuring against Moses as the Egyptian armed forces approached in full pursuit. To them, this was either sure of death or hostile re-enslavement. It's amazing how easily we forget the wonders God did yesterday just because a new challenge arises today, behaving as if it's too hard for God. News flash: God did what He did yesterday to let you know that what comes up today is nothing for Him to handle. The Israelites quickly forgot the awesome display of the might of God over the gods of the Egyptians and could not see beyond the Red Sea. Their vision was obscured by the obstacle that stood before them and their faith was unsettled by the enemy behind. But God, through the faith of Moses, brought them over.

Picture the vast host, numbering in the millions, looking out over the watery expanse, watching as pieces of chariots with the bodies of soldiers and horses drifted back onto the Egyptian shore. This overwhelming victory awoke the psalmist in Moses and he broke forth into singing. "Who is like the Lord?" A question which he asked in his song:

> *Exodus 15:11*
> *Who is like unto thee, O LORD, among the gods? Who is like thee, glorious in holiness, fearful in praises, doing wonders?*

This is echoed in the book of the Psalms as the writer reflects on the glorious nature of God:

> *Psalms 113:5*
> *Who is like unto the LORD our God, who dwelleth on high...*

There is absolutely none to be compared with our God. He is the creator of the heavens and the earth. The universe is His by virtue of creation. He fashioned man in His image and after His likeness; not like the gods of the earth created by men and fashioned after an image in their minds; idols which have eyes, ears, mouths, hands and feet but cannot see, hear, speak, act or move.

The men who create and worship them have to move them. Not so with Jehovah! We don't move Him; rather, He moves us, hallelujah!

He is indeed glorious in holiness; He is fearful in praises and great are the wonders He performs. The Bible is a treasure chest brimming with revelations of who God is; of His nature and character; of His wonder working power; of the greatness of His unconditional love and of the glory of His Kingdom and the benefits made available to His citizens. But how often we miss the move of His hand and lose out on the experience of His glory. So great is the number of those who have laid claim to salvation yet struggle unnecessarily with hardships, afflictions, sorrows, you name it. And even the hardships which might have been necessary are prolonged way beyond their allotted time because many people in the Body of Christ do not possess the key of knowledge that is required to unlock the doors to breakthroughs. It would seem that the word of God through the prophet Hosea is more relevant now than it has ever been at any point in history:

> *Hosea 4:6*
> *My people are destroyed for lack of knowledge: because thou hast rejected knowledge, I will also reject thee, that thou shalt be no priest to me: seeing thou hast forgotten the law of thy God, I will also forget thy children.*

It has often been said that what you don't know won't hurt you. That's a very dangerous belief for anyone to foster. What you don't know can very well destroy you. If you don't know your rights, how will you enjoy the benefits that are available for you to access? If you don't know the level of your authority, how can you exercise it? If you don't know what belongs to you, how can you claim it? The scriptures contain all the information that is necessary for us, not just to live, but to live effectively and abundantly in this life. It is not just a compilation of stories and letters. It is the constitution of the Kingdom of God; a legally binding document which furnishes us with everything we need to live lives that are in keeping with the principles and precepts of God's government.

> *2 Timothy 3:16-17*
> *16 All scripture is given by inspiration of God, and is profitable for doctrine, for reproof, for correction, for instruction in righteousness:*
> *17 That the man of God may be perfect, thoroughly furnished unto all good works.*

The aim of this book is to bring to light, some of the revelations - the gems contained in this treasure chest we call the Bible and properly adorn ourselves for Kingdom living. As we delve into the Word of God, examining specific scriptures from their languages of origin, that is, Hebrew and Greek, we explore the nature of God as King, the power of our praise, the power of agreement, the ability we have to condition our conditions, understanding the weight of glory imparted to us as Christ's ambassadors in the earth and the authority vested in us to do Kingdom business. May our knowledge increase and our understanding be expanded and may we access greater dimensions of the King's glory with the keys He has entrusted to us through His Word.

King of Kings
of Kings

KING OF KINGS OF KINGS

It was June 24, 1779, a date which has gone down in history as the beginning of the Great Siege. The Spanish and French were determined to regain control of the Rock of Gibraltar, the fortress which guarded the entrance to the Mediterranean, which was ceded in a treaty to the British. General George Augustus Elliott stood in command of five thousand three hundred and eighty two troops who committed themselves to defend the garrison against a Spanish force of thirteen thousand seven hundred and forty nine soldiers. The British were not daunted. Their morale was high. This type of siege was not uncommon to them. The Spanish and the French had tried time and time again to dominate the Rock, but to no avail.

By September of 1782, the British troops received reinforcements, increasing their numbers to seven thousand five hundred, but so did their rivals. According to some sources, they amassed a legion of thirty five thousand Spanish and eight thousand French fighters, outnumbering the British by an overwhelming majority. The British artillery consisted of ninety six guns and twelve gun boats while their enemies flaunted eighty six land guns, forty seven ships of line along with several gunboats and ten floating batteries. Yet with all this fire power, the attempts of the Spanish and French proved futile. Gibraltar was a mighty fortress; it was simply impenetrable, and in the end, the British celebrated a decisive victory.

As citizens of the Kingdom of God, we have a fortress more impenetrable than the Rock of Gibraltar. It's not a physical location. It cannot be identified on any map. Its coordinates are plotted in the realm of the Spirit and mention is made of it in the reservoir of the wisdom of Solomon in the book of Proverbs:

> *Proverbs 18:10*
> *The name of the LORD is a strong tower: the righteous runneth into it, and is safe.*

The word "name" comes from the Hebrew word "shêm" which refers not only to the label by which a person is called or identified, but also speaks of the reputation, fame, honour, authority and character of the individual. The Bible provides us with a multitude of names and titles by which God is known. The definition of each name and title gives us a knowledge of His nature, character and authority.

He is Elohim: *God*
He is Adonai: *Lord, Master, Owner*
He is El Elyon: *The Most High God*
He is El Shaddai: *God Almighty*
He is Jehovah Jireh: *The Lord Will Provide*

He is Jehovah Shalom: *The Lord Is Peace*
He is Jehovah Nissi: *The Lord Is My Banner*
He is Jehovah Shamma: *The Lord Is There*
He is Jehovah Rapha: *The Lord Who Heals*
He is Jehovah Sabaoth: *The Lord Of Hosts*
He is Jehovah Makkadesh: *The Lord Sanctifies*
He is Jehovah Rohi: *The Lord My Shepherd*
He is Jehovah Tsidkenu: *The Lord My Righteousness*

The above list is by no means exhaustive, just a fraction of the names and titles by which God is known in scripture. There is a side to God's nature that responds to every malady, every need, every circumstance we could possibly face. Grasping this leads us to understand that even the negative, undesirable situations that we deal with in this life, serve a divine purpose. You see, it's so easy to get stuck with a limited perception of who God is... some people just know Him as "God" and nothing else. Each negative situation provides us with a fresh, new revelation of who He is. If it wasn't for what the doctors told you, you would have never known that God is Jehovah Rapha: The Lord Who Heals. Had it not been for the time your landlord served you those eviction papers or when the bank threatened to repossess your car, you would have never known God as Jehovah Jireh: The Lord Provides. Do you remember when that relationship ended and you felt like the whole world turned its back on you? That's the time you realised that God is Jehovah Shamma: The Lord Who Is Always There. And who was it that died again? Man, that almost tore you to pieces. But in the midst of it, you had an unexplainable, indescribable peace. That's because God was there, letting you know that He is Jehovah Shalom: The Lord Is Peace. What an awesome God. While other religions embrace a polytheistic culture, having a different God for every different need, within the Kingdom of God, He that is Sovereign over us declares Himself to be "I Am That I Am", I Am self-existent; whatever you need, it's contained in Me; I can be Who I choose to be at whatever time I choose! Hallelujah!

According to Solomon in Proverbs 18:10, who has the right to benefit from the awesome glory of the Lord's name? The righteous. The word "righteous" comes from the Hebrew "tsaddîyq" which refers to one who has been justified and vindicated by God; one who is just and right in his cause, in judgment and character and is in right standing with government. How can one expect to claim the right to healing, provision, peace, contentment, forgiveness or any other benefit of the Kingdom of God when the lifestyle of such a one is in contradiction to the constitution of the Kingdom? The power of the Name is for those who are in right standing with the Name.

When the righteous runs into the strong tower, the refuge, the fortress of the name of the Lord, no matter what enemy, what force, what opposition it is that was in pursuit, the name of the Lord is a wall of fire, an impenetrable stronghold which provides a safe haven for its inhabitants that no other can provide. The word "safe" comes from the Hebrew word "sâgab" which means to be inaccessibly high; to be too high for capture; to be high in prosperity; to be set securely on high; to be exalted to the place where hostility becomes ineffective. Oh glory, hallelujah! What a blessed assurance. When we run into the security of the name of the Lord, we are taken to a height that the enemy cannot pursue... their best efforts become ineffective; we become inaccessible to their greatest machinations.

Among the names and titles of God declared to us through the Word, there is one that sums up who He is, encompassing His power, might, dignity, glory, royalty and sovereignty along with His nature and character. It is the title: KING. According to the dictionaries of choice, a king is a male ruler of a country who usually inherits his position and rules for life, further explaining that he comes into position upon the death of the previous monarch; his position is hereditary and passes to his successor at the time of his death or if he abdicates the throne. Now, we cannot rightly apply this definition to the kingship of God. For one, He did not inherit His kingship. There was no one for Him to inherit it from. He existed before existence came to exist. He did not just begin the beginning... He is the beginning. There are no successors lined up to take over rulership from Him. He is from everlasting to everlasting. His dominion endures forever.

> *Psalms 90:2*
> *Before the mountains were brought forth, or ever thou hadst formed the earth and the world, even from everlasting to everlasting, thou art God.*

> *Psalms 93:1-2*
> *1 The LORD reigneth, he is clothed with majesty; the LORD is clothed with strength, wherewith he hath girded himself: the world also is stablished, that it cannot be moved.*
> *2 Thy throne is established of old: thou art from everlasting.*

> *Psalms 145:13*
> *Thy kingdom is an everlasting kingdom, and thy dominion endureth throughout all generations.*

Our King will never relinquish His sovereign authority; He will never abdicate His throne, nor can He ever be overthrown. Edward II was crowned king of England in 1307 following the death of his father, Edward I. In 1308 he married Isabella of France, the daughter of the powerful French monarch, King Philip IV, in an attempt to resolve long running tensions between the two crowns. Leap forward to the latter end of his reign... In 1325, with his marriage in turmoil due to his misdeeds and illicit activities, King Edward II sent his queen to France to negotiate a treaty, but instead, she formed an alliance with an enemy of the British throne, amassed a small army and launched a coup d'état against her husband, causing the king to flee his own kingdom in search of safe haven. The unwavering persistence of Isabella and her allies awarded them the winning move. Edward II was captured not long after and forced to abdicate his throne. Upon being sentenced to imprisonment, his son, Edward III was enthroned in his stead and Isabella installed as regent.

History teems with accounts like this. There have been many successful coups against thrones and governments; a stark reminder of how fickle human rulership and authority really is. Yet, when we check our records, there has only been one attempt, one failed attempt at dethroning the King of Kings. You remember that fellow they used to call Lucifer? He no longer goes by that name though. He's now Satan. His failed coup won him a life sentence - eternity in hell. Isaiah tells us about it:

> *Isaiah 14:12-15*
> *12 How art thou fallen from heaven, O Lucifer, son of the morning! how art thou cut down to the ground, which didst weaken the nations!*

> *13 For thou hast said in thine heart, I will ascend into heaven, I will exalt my throne above the stars of God: I will sit also upon the mount of the congregation, in the sides of the north:*
> *14 I will ascend above the heights of the clouds; I will be like the most High.*
> *15 Yet thou shalt be brought down to hell, to the sides of the pit.*

In one of my favourite verses, Psalm 29:10, David makes it clear that God's rule is not just expressed over the affairs of man, neither is He just Governor among the nations, but nature itself is subject to His kingly authority.

> *Psalms 29:10*
> *The LORD sitteth upon the flood; yea, the LORD sitteth King for ever.*

A flood refers to an overflowing of the land by water; a deluge. In a flood, land and vegetation are at the mercy of the raging waters. The best hope is for a quick subsidence of the overwhelming torrents. I remember in my younger days my friends and I would walk a couple miles to get to the Wag Water River in St. Mary, Jamaica. We would spend the day fishing and swimming. We knew the best fishing spots, one of which was at the mouth where the river enters the sea. There were times during the year when we had torrential rainfall. Wag Water would overflow its banks and the force of the water would tear away land and trees, rerouting the flow of water at some points. It was sometimes most noticeable at the mouth where the flood would deliver perhaps tons of sand, stones and dirt, creating an embankment, shifting the location where the water empties into the sea by several feet.

When the Bible speaks of floods, it is sometimes used symbolically to refer to troubles, trials, hardships. God sits as King upon the flood. No matter how the waters may rage; no matter how the troubles, trials and hardships may surge and shift the natural course of life, as long as our King remains enthroned upon the troubled waters, they can never shift us out of His divine will for our lives. As a matter of fact, they will only serve to push us to our destination in quicker time. Have you ever noticed that everything moves downstream much faster than usual whenever flooding takes place? Not only that, but no matter how the course of the river may change, it always empties out where it should - in the sea. Every flood you face as a citizen of the Kingdom of God is under the control of your King. They might shift your expected path but they cannot, and I repeat, cannot change your ordained destination.

There are several places in scripture where God is titled not just as King, but as King of Kings, indicating that his dominion is so glorious that other kings are subject to Him. He is a King above those kings, and rightly so.

> *1 Timothy 6:15*
> *Which in his times he shall shew, who is the blessed and only Potentate, the King of kings, and Lord of lords;*

> *Revelation 17:14*
> *These shall make war with the Lamb, and the Lamb shall overcome them: for he is Lord of lords, and King of kings: and they that are with him are called, and chosen, and faithful.*

> *Revelation 19:16*
> *And he hath on his vesture and on his thigh a name written, KING OF KINGS, AND LORD OF LORDS.*

But this is not a title which is ascribed to God alone. There were other earthly kings in scripture which received the same ascription. Artaxerxes in Ezra 7:12 and Nebuchadnezzar in Ezekiel 26:7 and Daniel 2:37 were both esteemed as such. Even Solomon, the third king of Israel, blessed with understanding and wealth far above his fellows. Though the title may not have been verbally attributed, it was evident that he was thus honoured in the fact that the kings of the surrounding nations paid tribute to him yearly. In more recent times, there were several rulers who rose to such a rank. Among them was Ramesses II, also known as Ramesses the Great, revered as one of the greatest pharaohs of Egypt. He died at the age of ninety six years and had over two hundred wives and concubines with ninety six sons and sixty daughters. His reign was so long that the Egyptians feared that when he died the world would have come to an end. Well, that was quite a number of centuries ago and the sun still rises in the east and sets in the west.

Another was Tigranes II, the king of kings of Armenian history. He conquered some of the greatest powers of his time and through his successful exploits, his kingdom thrived. It is said that whenever he ventured into public space, he always had at least four kings attending to him. At the age of seventy five he still engaged in active warfare against Roman legions. He died of old age at the age of eighty five. Cyrus the Great of Persia also bore the title as well as Alexander the Great who succeeded the Persian kings.

Each of these highly exalted rulers differ from each other in their style of rulership, their exploits and even the reach of their authority as some rose to higher levels of prominence than others. Yet, they all had one thing in common: as great as they were, they all had to fall prostrate before death. They were all uncrowned by the grave.

Upon examining the matter, the Jews became unsettled in their minds that the Only Wise God was addressed in the same manner as mortal men whose reign was so limited. They began addressing God with a new title, a Hebrew appellation: "Melech Malchei HaMelachim". The English translation is: "King of Kings of Kings". He is not just a King above other kings; He is indeed the King who rules over all other kings of kings. What a glorious day when every knee shall bow and every tongue shall confess that He is Lord. Just imagine Ramesses II, Tigranes II, Cyrus, Alexander, Nebuchadnezzar, Artaxerxes, Solomon and every other king of the earth, rising up from their slumber, falling to their knees and confessing with their own mouths that "Jehovah, the Creator of Heaven and earth, the Great Almighty God truly is the Supreme King."

The ultimate role of a king is to secure the welfare of his citizens. He gives no place to selfish ambitions. The well-being of the people of his kingdom becomes foremost in his will and every command, decree and statute is made toward this end. The state of his kingdom literally hangs on the thread of his integrity. So long as he possesses the true heart of a king and his will swings toward the interest of the citizens, their welfare is ensured, but, if he chooses to embrace selfish ambitions then his people suffer. It is by no means an easy feat to wield such power and authority. Many rulers in history have worn the title of king but at heart they were dictators and tyrants, oppressing their own citizens, bleeding their kingdoms dry and leaving a throne embroiled in turmoil and chaos to their successors. But how blessed is the assurance that our King has never been and will never be numbered among dictators and tyrants. The heart that He had for His citizens at the time of creation is the same heart He possesses today. His will has not changed. His love has not diminished. His compassion has not dwindled. His Word proves it:

> *Malachi 3:6*
> *For I am the LORD, I change not; therefore ye sons of Jacob are not consumed.*

> *James 1:17*
> *Every good gift and every perfect gift is from above, and cometh down from the Father of lights, with whom is no variableness, neither shadow of turning.*

A king expresses his authority and imposes his will through his commands. When he speaks, his words carry the effect of law. His decrees and declarations are carried out with swiftness and without question:

> *Ecclesiastes 8:4*
> *Where the word of a king is, there is power: and who may say unto him, What doest thou?*

The authority of earthly kings is limited to the region over which they exert influence. Their commands are effective so long as they are issued within their scope of influence. The king of France could not command the citizens of England; neither could the king of England command the citizens of France. Why? Because the scope of their influence only permitted them to command those within their own realm. Citizens move at the command of their own kings, not at the command of the kings of foreign nations.

There is no limit to the authority of the King of Kings of Kings. His commands transcend earthly boundaries and time zones. Heavenly bodies: the sun, moon and stars align themselves in obedience to the sound of His voice. He speaks where there is nothing and even the very nothingness obeys Him and becomes the very thing that He speaks. The words of His mouth cause non-existence to become pregnant with existence as He calls the things which are not as though they were. He sat enthroned at the time of creation and commanded the dark, empty expanse to give birth to the universe. He spoke into chaos and order manifested. His voice thundered with authority and majesty: "Let there be", and without hesitation or question, there was. He set His decrees in place to govern creation, establishing the cycles of life, the principles of production and reproduction which have flowed in continuance from generation to generation for thousands of years. No man can interrupt what He has established; not even the devil himself can break His ordinances. Whatever He has commanded concerning your life, it shall come to pass; you shall see and experience the manifestation of it. He is not like man that He should lie or the son of man that He should repent. Whatever He spoke about you, you shall see it! Your healing, your blessing, your breakthrough, your miracle, your joy, your contentment, your peace of mind, your success are not just benefits, they are laws. Your King said it, therefore it shall be done. What He has spoken, He shall perform. The world and all that dwell therein, the universe and all it contains, are at His disposal. Conditions, situations and circumstances are being shifted and rearranged in your favour. Earthly rulers and even the opposition who rules over the kingdom of darkness cannot hinder what God is doing on your behalf. The command concerning your life has already been issued by the Melech Malchei HaMelachim: The KING OF KINGS OF KINGS.

1 Timothy 1:17
Now unto the King eternal, immortal, invisible, the only wise God, be honour and glory for ever and ever. Amen.

His Train

Fills

The Temple

HIS TRAIN FILLS THE TEMPLE

The Bible, from beginning to end, all sixty six books, is pregnant with mysteries and revelations. The book of Isaiah is replete with such revelations wrapped up in the prophetic promises of God uttered by the Old Testament prophet. Let's unwrap chapter 6 and see what the verses give birth to.

Isaiah 6:1-8
1 In the year that king Uzziah died I saw also the Lord sitting upon a throne, high and lifted up, and his train filled the temple.
2 Above it stood the seraphims: each one had six wings; with twain he covered his face, and with twain he covered his feet, and with twain he did fly.
3 And one cried unto another, and said, Holy, holy, holy, is the LORD of hosts: the whole earth is full of his glory.
4 And the posts of the door moved at the voice of him that cried, and the house was filled with smoke.
5 Then said I, Woe is me! for I am undone; because I am a man of unclean lips, and I dwell in the midst of a people of unclean lips: for mine eyes have seen the King, the LORD of hosts.
6 Then flew one of the seraphims unto me, having a live coal in his hand, which he had taken with the tongs from off the altar:

> *7 And he laid it upon my mouth, and said, Lo, this hath touched thy lips; and thine iniquity is taken away, and thy sin purged.*
> *8 Also I heard the voice of the Lord, saying, Whom shall I send, and who will go for us? Then said I, Here am I; send me.*

Isaiah begins the chapter by stating what happened and giving the timeline of when it happened. In the very same year that Uzziah, who was king over Judah at the time, died, he had a divine encounter with God. From chapter one to five, Isaiah was preaching and recounting the visions that God gave him to the people of Judah. But now, the God whom he preached about for five chapters was about to reveal Himself to him.

In this spectacular visitation, Isaiah beheld God sitting on a throne. Who sits on a throne? A king! In the same year that the earthly king with whom he had grown accustomed died, Isaiah came in contact with the Almighty, Everlasting, Omnipotent King of Kings. Not only was He sitting on a throne but He was also high and lifted up. He was elevated and exalted to a level of royalty and majesty far beyond the kings of the nations of the earth.

What was the next thing that the preacher saw? "His train filled the temple". This simple phrase holds so much weight and potency. When you understand and embrace this it shifts your perspective of every condition you face and positions you in certain victory over every attack of the enemy. HIS TRAIN FILLED THE TEMPLE. In the Old Testament era when the nations were ruled by kings, the ultimate aim of every king was to expand his kingdom. The only way a kingdom could expand was through conquest. Kings would wage war against each other from time to time and the champion of the war would take control of the territory of his opponent, putting the citizens under servitude and thus expanding his kingdom. Now, there was a custom that the kings of that era observed. They wore robes with trains which was a long flowing piece of garment which trailed him as he walked. Whenever a king became victorious in battle, he would cut off a piece of the losing king's train and attach it to his, making his train longer. But it also served another purpose. If you were privileged to stand before that king and you wanted to know how many wars he won, you wouldn't have to ask him. All you had to do was count the pieces of trains stitched onto his. If you counted five pieces, it means he won five wars; if you counted ten pieces it means he won ten wars... you get the picture.

Now, Isaiah said that God's train "filled" the temple. The edifice in that time was constructed under the rulership of King Solomon who had received the blueprint, directives and even the provision of resources from his father King David. The entire dimension of the temple, taking in the outer court, inner court and all other areas, was no small matter. It was designed to accommodate thousands of people during times of worship. For God's train to have filled the temple, covering the length and breadth of that massive structure, it simply means that every single battle the enemy has waged against His people from the beginning of time until now; and even the wars that you have not yet faced, God has already won the victory on your behalf. Every attack against your finances, your health, your family, your job, your marriage, your home, your ministry, your peace of mind, your victory has already been secured by God and He has the train to prove it. Hallelujah! This is why Moses proclaimed loudly:

> *Exodus 15:3*
> *The LORD is a man of war: the LORD is his name.*

And Isaiah relays the same sentiments:

> *Isaiah 42:13*
> *The LORD shall go forth as a mighty man, he shall stir up jealousy like a man of war: he shall cry, yea, roar; he shall prevail against his enemies.*

The words of the prophet Jahaziel seals it perfectly as he prophesied in 2 Chronicles 20:15. It was when Moab, Ammon and Mount Seir came up against Judah. Jehoshaphat who was king of Judah found himself between a rock and a hard place. He called the nation together to fast for God's intervention and as he finished praying, the prophet stood up and declared: "the battle is not yours, it belongs to God; you will not need to fight in this battle, stand still and see the salvation of the Lord."

Be assured my friend, that the warfare you see before you right now is just a delayed broadcast of an event for which God has already won the victory from before the foundation of the world. Whatever the nature of that warfare is, there's a piece of train on God's robe with your victory written on it.

In verse two, Isaiah continues his analytic description of what he saw in his divine encounter. Above the throne of the King he saw seraphim (plural for the word "seraph") which were angels who attended to the throne of God in constant worship. Each of these angels had six wings. They covered their faces with two, they covered their feet with two and they used the other two to fly. What was taking place here? This was worship in reverence and humility.

There was a custom in eastern kingdoms in ancient times which required that whenever the king left the royal confines of the palace and walked in public in the presence of his citizens, the people would cover their faces and their feet and any other part of the body which would have been exposed, being careful to ensure that only the eyes were left uncovered to see the king as he passed by, and as he did, they would bow and worship him. The covering of the body parts was to them, the utmost show of reverence.

Here we have the seraphim covering themselves displaying the utmost reverence for the Most High God. In addition to their humble reverence, they gave voice to their worship, shouting "holy, holy, holy, is the LORD of Hosts: the whole earth is full of His glory". This pattern of worship was also witnessed by John as recorded in the book of Revelation when he was exiled on the Isle of Patmos:

> *Revelation 4:8*
> *And the four beasts had each of them six wings about him; and they were full of eyes within: and they rest not day and night, saying, Holy, holy, holy, Lord God Almighty, which was, and is, and is to come.*

Now, worship is not just something that a king is worthy of; worship also entertains the king. And when a king is entertained, there is always reciprocity. Whenever a king blesses a subject, it is always of a far greater proportion than what was presented to him first. Remember when the Queen of Sheba entertained Solomon with her gifts (1 Kings 10)? What he gave her in return was far more than what she presented to him.

Remember when the daughter of Herodias entertained Herod on his birthday with a dance (Matthew 14)? He was so enthralled that he promised to grant her request, up to half of the kingdom. Can you just imagine what Heaven releases when we entertain the sovereign King with our worship? There is always a release of glory. Sometimes it manifests in a physical, tangible way. Other times it manifests in the realm of the spirit, affecting situations and conditions that we deal with in the natural. Where am I going with this? Isaiah states the result of the angelic worship which he witnessed in the temple. He said "And the posts of the door moved at the voice of him that cried, and the house was filled with smoke."

The word "moved" in that verse comes from the Hebrew "nuwa", which means literally to shake, quiver, totter, tremble, vibrate. What was taking place? It was an earthquake. So powerful was the worship being offered up that it disturbed the very foundation of the physical structure and the evidence of the glory was there as well... the temple was filled with smoke. My God! If we only knew the dynamic glory lingering in the heavenlies waiting to be unleashed to shake the foundations of hell that come against us!

It was not just the physical structure that was impacted by the shaking that occurred; the foundation of Isaiah's heart was also greatly moved. So great was the magnitude of the shaking he experienced that he exclaimed:

"Woe is me! For I am undone; because I am a man of unclean lips, and I dwell in the midst of a people of unclean lips: for mine eyes have seen the King, the LORD of hosts."

"Woe is me... I am doomed!" What an exclamation by the prophet. His awesome, yet frightful encounter with the Almighty drove him to a state of terror. He witnessed the holy presence of God and heard the angels proclaiming His holiness. Then the divine, unadulterated holiness of God magnified to Isaiah, his own unholiness. When we see God for who He truly is, then we see ourselves for who we truly are and we see where we truly stand. Isaiah became aware of his sinful state and saw that he was on no higher a plain than the people to whom he had preached the message of repentance for the first five chapters of the book attributed to him. He knew full well that no unholiness can stand in the holy presence of the King, hence his exclamation, "woe is me!" The truth is that oftentimes, because God in His sovereignty chooses to use us to minister in whatever manner to His people, we mistakenly feel that we are somehow in greater standing than them. Oh, if we would only just realise that oftentimes we suffer from the same diagnosis as the people to whom we are sent with the prescription.

It would do us great good to swallow a dose of the medicine ourselves before meting out dosages to others. So often the people we are sent to, swallow theirs with humility and are changed for the better while we are left nursing our ailments, still foolishly presuming that we are more spiritually well off than them.

Another thing that must happen when we have a real encounter with God is that our perception of Him must change. There must be a graduation to a higher level in our revelation of Him. "So when did this happen with Isaiah?" you may ask. It's right there in verse five. Isaiah called God "LORD". "But he has been calling Him Lord all along," you may protest. Yes, indeed, but watch keenly. He calls Him Lord in verse one... "I saw also the Lord". The word rendered there is "Adônây" which was the general name used by the Hebrews when referring to or calling on the name of the Lord in the Old Testament. When he says "LORD" in verse five, the word rendered is "Yahweh", a name so sacredly revered that it was only used by the high priests when they ministered before the presence of God in the Holy of Holies. What took place? Isaiah's perception of God shifted. He began to see God not as everyone else saw Him. He began to see God for who He truly was. He began to see God in His splendour and majesty as the angels did... It was the same reference they used in verse three when they proclaimed "holy, holy, holy is the LORD". You can never behold the glory and remain the same!

The subsequent verses of the chapter detail the preparation and promotion of Isaiah to a higher calling. His ministry took on a new dimension. After becoming aware of his personal state, acknowledging it and making confession, one of the angels took a live coal, a burning coal from off the altar and laid it on his mouth. The altar was the place where sacrificial offerings were burnt before the Lord. The burning coal was taken from there and placed on the very source of his spiritual instability - his lips, his unclean lips. Isaiah literally became a living sacrifice. He demonstrated with his own life what Paul wrote about hundreds of years later in his letter to the Romans:

> *Romans 12:1*
> *I beseech you therefore, brethren, by the mercies of God, that ye present your bodies a living sacrifice, holy, acceptable unto God, which is your reasonable service.*

As children of God, especially for those who are called to ministry, we must understand that preparation precedes promotion. This is why many folks become stagnated after a while. They are greatly gifted; the evidence of the anointing is on them but they get stuck on one level, never advancing because of their own failure to prepare themselves for the next level.

Churches are closing and pastors are resigning at an alarming rate these days (how can one resign from the call of God?). The blame is being bounced around to various factors but all it comes down to, is a failure to prepare for the next level. Remember that the natural is a reflection of the spiritual. The principles and cycles established in the natural realm are indications of what takes place in the spiritual realm. Your boss would never promote you unless you qualify yourself for the promotion. So often, employees quarrel about the new person that got promoted over them even though they have been faithful to the boss for fifteen years. Reality check - years of service do not qualify you for promotion! Do you have what it takes to produce and perform at optimum level and handle the pressures of the next level? The promotion requires a degree. Did you take the time to upgrade yourself from the high school diploma or the college certificate you got so long ago? Are you prepared for it?

How then do we expect a God of principles and order to promote us to a higher calling when we don't take time to prepare our spiritual lives for what the next level requires. We want to prophesy but we use the same mouth to gossip. We want to lay hands on the sick and see them recover but those same hands dabble in mischief. We want to discern yet our eyes feast on pornography and our minds can only conceive envy and hatred. There has to be preparation before promotion.

There must be a cutting and stripping away of whatever the weights are that so easily beset us, whether they are habits or desires or even relationships. Face it friends, some folks are toxic to your advancement. Not all relationships will help to propel you to your next level. Some are weights which will only fasten you to where you are and cause you to become dormant and stagnant.

Isaiah leaves from a state of deep grief and despair; feeling doomed in the presence of the King with his sinful self, to a state of boldness, fervency and enthusiasm to be an ambassador of God to the nations. This was Isaiah's transition into prophetic ministry. For the first five chapters he was simply declaring a vision to the people and imploring them to repentance. After his encounter with God and his process of preparation, he now stood as not just a prophet, but has been recorded in Biblical history as one of the major prophets of the Old Testament.

The Spirit of God is calling you now to a higher level; a level of extended borders and expanded territory. All the struggles, pains, hurts, sorrows and hardships are just a part of the process of preparation for your transition. The assurance that you have is that no matter what battles the enemy wages against you, you have already been placed in a position of victory. Jehovah has already fought the battle and handed you the triumph and He has the train on His robe to prove it. The evidence is there! His train fills the temple.

There's A Lion
In Your
Praise

THERE'S A
LION IN YOUR PRAISE

The word declares that we should sing praises with understanding. What is it that we need to understand? Firstly, we must understand who God is. Who is He? He is the King of all the earth. Who is a King? A king is one who expresses sovereign rule over a region or territory. The region influenced by his rulership becomes his kingdom and he becomes lord over it. Note that word, "lord". We use it ever so often to refer to our God in our prayers, in worship, in conversation. The word "lord" means "owner". Therefore, when we call God "Lord", we are declaring that He is our owner.

Look at it this way... for those who live in rented property, every time the rent becomes due, who do you pay it to? Do you hand it to your neighbour? I think not. Do you put it in an envelope and bring it to church as offering? As noble as that sounds, that's not the reality. You hand it over to the landlord. The word landlord simply means land owner. Get it? So when we sing praises it should be done with the understanding first and foremost that we are singing to our God, our King, our Lord, our Owner!

Secondly, we must understand how to praise. Praise is not static or stationary. It is dynamic. Too often though, it is robbed of its dynamism because people get too traditional or one-tracked in their approach: "this is the way we've always done it in this church" or "this is the way my grandparents and my parents did it" and we end up singing the same songs, reading the same Psalms, shouting the same shout, dancing the same dance and doing everything the same way like a record stuck on replay. The Bible presents us with several Hebrew words which Bible scholars have termed "the seven levels of praise". These are found throughout Old Testament passages, each carrying a different meaning and each commanding a different posture in praise. They are as follows:

Type of Praise	Brief Description
Towdah	*To extend the hands in thanksgiving*
Yadah	*To offer praise by waving the hands; to cast or throw*
Tehillah	*To express praise through the singing of hymns and psalms*
Shabach	*To shout; address in a loud tone; to command; to triumph*
Zamar	*To pluck the string; to offer praise through music*

Halal	*To boast; celebrate; rave; be clamorously foolish*
Barak	*To kneel; bow; become prostrate; bless God as an act of adoration*

When we come into the presence of the King there are protocols that must be observed. Many people are satisfied with just singing the songs and getting their groove on with the music but if what we desire is to offer praise in spirit and in truth, praise that is worthy of the King and accepted by Him, then there are principles that must be adhered to. Praise is not a compilation of songs with sweet melody and tight harmony. It's an expression of adoration and thankfulness to the King for His faithfulness to us. Our praise is an offering being presented to God, the King of Kings of Kings; it must be presented in a manner worthy of royalty. How much care do we take on birthdays and special occasions to ensure that the gifts we present to our loved ones are properly packaged and beautifully wrapped, adorned with a bow and a card. How much more effort should we put into presenting our praise to our King?

In a psalm 100, one of David's hymns of doxology or Psalm of praise, whichever title you prefer to apply, we are presented with some key principles for approaching God in praise.

❖ *Psalms 100:1*
Make a joyful noise unto the LORD, all ye lands.

Appear before the King with a jubilant, celebratory attitude. Our praise should be underlined with joy and cheerfulness. The phrase "joyful noise" is derived from the Hebrew word "rûwa" which means to shout; to split the ears with sound; to give a blast; to shout in triumph over the enemy. We appear before Him not with a defeatist mentality, but as people returning from battle in triumph.

❖ *Psalms 100:2*
Serve the LORD with gladness: come before his presence with singing.

The word "serve" is the Hebrew "âbad" meaning to do service; to be a worshipper. As we offer our praise and worship to God it should be with gladness, glee, mirth, pleasure, rejoicing. We also need to understand that our praise is not restricted to a few minutes of music, shouting, singing and dancing. Whatever we do concerning the King is an expression of our reverence to Him. How we do what we do indicates the level of adoration we have for Him; it's an expression of praise. We are implored to serve Him with gladness; do His service with gladness of heart.

> ❖ *Psalms 100:3*
> *Know ye that the LORD he is God: it is he that hath made us, and not we ourselves; we are his people, and the sheep of his pasture.*

Know who God is and who we are in relation to Him. The Lord is God. David tells us to know this. In the Hebrew, the word "know" goes beyond simply having head knowledge about something. It carries a connotation of an intimate relationship. To know that the Lord is God is to have an intimate, personal connection with Him, not knowing about Him based on somebody else's testimony. It's to see Him, feel Him and experience Him for yourself. We enter into praise with that level of intimacy. Having an intimate knowledge of Him then leads us to knowing that we belong to Him; He created us. He is our Lord, our Owner. He also assumes the role of our Shepherd, our Guide, our Director, our Keeper. When we know the King, we praise Him with confidence regardless of the outer conditions that prevail around us. We know that He is the God that has never lost a war. He is the King of Glory, El Gibbor, the Mighty God, the God who is mighty in battle

When we know the King intimately, we also know what He requires. He is a holy God and therefore requires that we likewise be holy (1 Peter 1:16). He is righteous and requires of us that we be righteous also, which means to be in right standing with Him. How can we expect our praise to be accepted by Him when the lifestyle from which the praise flows is contrary to His character? It is from this knowledge base that David expressed in Psalm 66:18 that if we regard iniquity in our hearts the Lord will not hear us. Remember His command concerning offerings in the Old Testament? Anything being presented to Him must be in mint condition, without spot or blemish; clean and wholesome. This is how we should strive to present our praise to Him - in mint condition. If our lives are contaminated, then so will our praise be.

❖ *Psalms 100:4*
Enter into his gates with thanksgiving, and into his courts with praise: be thankful unto him, and bless his name.

We approach the King with gratitude. Express our appreciation for what He has already done, what He is doing and what He has promised to do, knowing assuredly that if He promised it, He will bring it to pass. This particular verse is loaded with four of the seven levels of praise. Firstly, David says "thanksgiving" which in the Hebrew is "tôwdâh" which instructs us to extend the hands in thanksgiving to God. Secondly, he uses the word "praise" which comes from "tehillâh" which instructs us to express praise through hymns or psalms". Thirdly, he says "thankful", which in Hebrew is "yâdâh", speaking of praising God with the waving of the hands in a manner resembling throwing a stone or an arrow. Fourthly, he says "bless" which is derived from the Hebrew word "bârak" which implies kneeling or becoming prostrate before God in praise and adoration as we salute Him.

> ❖ *Psalms 100:5*
> *For the LORD is good; his mercy is everlasting; and his truth endureth to all generations.*

Here the hymn concludes by declaring why we should praise as we ought to praise. We praise him for His goodness, His unchangeable goodness. No matter how things change, no matter how times change, no matter how people change, God remains constant. He is unmovable, unshakable. From everlasting to everlasting He remains the same. Our King is not one to adapt to changing times and conditions; He is not one to adjust His character to suit situations. When He begins to move, times and conditions adapt to Him and situations shift to accommodate His perfect will. He doesn't just possess truth, He is Truth. This is why His truth endures - it is who He is.

Thirdly, we must understand the effects of our praise. To get this understanding let's go all the way back to the beginning, the book of Genesis. Many of us might be familiar with the account of Jacob and how he deceived his father and stole his brother's birth right; how his father implored him to go to Padanaram to marry one of Laban's daughters; how he fell in love with Rachel, the younger of Laban's two daughters; how he pledged to work seven years for Laban in return for the right to marry her; how Laban tricked him and caused him to marry Leah, the older sister instead; how he worked for yet another seven years just to marry the woman that he truly loved. Let's pick up this account from Genesis 29:31.

> *Genesis 29:31-35*
> *31 And when the LORD saw that Leah was hated, he opened her womb: but Rachel was barren.*
> *32 And Leah conceived, and bare a son, and she called his name Reuben: for she said, Surely the LORD hath looked upon my affliction; now therefore my husband will love me.*
> *33 And she conceived again, and bare a son; and said, Because the LORD hath heard that I was hated, he hath therefore given me this son also: and she called his name Simeon.*
> *34 And she conceived again, and bare a son; and said, Now this time will my husband be joined unto me, because I have born him three sons: therefore was his name called Levi.*
> *35 And she conceived again, and bare a son: and she said, Now will I praise the LORD: therefore she called his name Judah; and left bearing.*

Notice the pattern with Leah. She finds herself in a relationship in which she is basically unloved and unwanted. She starts having children for her husband. The first son she brings forth, she names him Reuben which means "He (the Lord) has seen my affliction". What you should pay attention to is the reason behind the name... "now my husband will love me".

She then has another son and names this one Simeon, meaning "He (God) hears". Her reasoning was that because God has heard that I'm not loved then He's giving me this son so that my husband will begin to love me.

Son number three comes and he receives the name Levi. The meaning of this name is "joined". In her heart she believed exactly what she said in the verse, that her husband would be joined or drawn close to her because now she has given him three sons.

Here comes son number four. After having the first three, nothing has changed in Jacob's feelings toward her. She names him Judah which means "praise". Her husband's attitude did not change toward her but look at the change in her attitude. Previously, it was all about winning the love of a man who couldn't care less about her, but here she says "now I will praise the Lord!" Wow! What a shift. Let's step back for a second here. How many times do we squeeze ourselves into Leah's shoes, trying to win the fleeting approval, or affection of someone else? Often times compromising our standards and even our salvation just for the attention of another mere mortal, be it a supervisor or a boss or a partner. Understand this my friend, that for every door that God allows us to walk through, every relationship He allows us to enter, every job He blesses us to work in, the attitude should not be "how can I win their approval or affection or attention" rather, "how can God get PRAISE through this".

Let's get back on course here. In Genesis 49, Jacob is now at the point of death and begins to carry out a tradition passed down through the generations. He is about to pronounce a blessing upon each of his sons. You see, in those days, the blessings conferred by a father upon his children especially at the point of death carried great prophetic weight. Once uttered, it became irreversible. We saw this in the case of Isaac in the blessing he pronounced upon Jacob (Genesis 27). No amount of weeping from Esau, the rightful heir, could reverse the blessing even though it was the "wrong" son who received the pronouncement.

As was tradition, Jacob blesses his sons in order beginning with the eldest. He now gets to Judah.

> *Genesis 49:9-10*
> *9 Judah is a lion's whelp: from the prey, my son, thou art gone up: he stooped down, he couched as a lion, and as an old lion; who shall rouse him up?*
> *10 The sceptre shall not depart from Judah, nor a lawgiver from between his feet, until Shiloh come; and unto him shall the gathering of the people be.*

Note carefully the words he pronounces over Judah. He calls him a lion's whelp or a young lion. Then he says in verse 10, that the sceptre which signified kingship or royal rule, shall always be in the tribe or lineage of Judah and there will always be a succession of lawgivers, referring to kings, until Shiloh come. Who was Shiloh? Shiloh was the Messiah, Jesus Christ!

So potent was the blessing upon Judah that even hundreds of years after Judah himself died, the word was still living and active, arranging and rearranging, ordering and reordering people, conditions and situations for its manifestation. Remember who the first king of Israel was? Yeah, it was Saul. But Saul was not from the tribe of Judah. He was from the tribe of Benjamin. Kingship was not pronounced upon his lineage. He had to lose his position. It was not really his to begin with. He was just a placeholder because David, who was from the tribe of Judah, was not fully ready yet to come into kingship. But just stand in awe at the wisdom of God. The Sovereign Lord simply allowed Saul to establish the kingdom, set up the army and organise the government in preparation for David's coronation. And there you are getting all flustered and depressed because you haven't seen what God has promised yet. You haven't seen it yet because He's allowing somebody else to do the ground work. How else can you inherit houses you never built and vineyards you never planted? Someone else has to build them and plant them so that when you arrive all you have to do is occupy.

The blessing pronounced on Judah was so on point that even when the nation of Israel had split with the tribes of Judah and Benjamin forming the nation of Judah and the other ten tribes forming the nation of Israel, right throughout the generations, there was always royalty in Judah.

At the birth of the New Testament era, as Heaven was getting ready to release Shiloh, the Messiah, Jesus Christ the Son of the Living God into the earth, the eyes of Israel and of others who understood Old Testament prophecy were fixed on the house or lineage of Judah. And sure enough, Judah was the gateway through which He entered the earth realm. Take a look at what Matthew says:

> *Matthew 1:1-3*
> *1 The book of the generation of Jesus Christ, the son of David, the son of Abraham.*
> *2 Abraham begat Isaac; and Isaac begat Jacob; and Jacob begat Judas and his brethren;*
> *3 And Judas begat Phares and Zara of Thamar; and Phares begat Esrom; and Esrom begat Aram;*

The name Judas there in verses three and four is the Greek equivalent of the Hebrew 'Judah'; the very same Judah to whom his father, Jacob prophesied hundreds of years before. And right there, in that very same lineage, we see Jesus Christ, the Messiah, the Shiloh, the Son of the Living God who was the subject of Judah's prophetic promise.

Let's fast forward to the book of Revelation. The prophecy was given in the book of beginnings (Genesis) and the completion is seen in the book of endings (Revelation).

> *Revelation 5:1-5*
> *1 And I saw in the right hand of him that sat on the throne a book written within and on the backside, sealed with seven seals.*
> *2 And I saw a strong angel proclaiming with a loud voice, Who is worthy to open the book, and to loose the seals thereof?*
> *3 And no man in heaven, nor in earth, neither under the earth, was able to open the book, neither to look thereon.*
> *4 And I wept much, because no man was found worthy to open and to read the book, neither to look thereon.*
> *5 And one of the elders saith unto me, Weep not: behold, the Lion of the tribe of Juda, the Root of David, hath prevailed to open the book, and to loose the seven seals thereof.*

Pay keen attention to verse five. Look at the title ascribed to Jesus: "THE LION OF THE TRIBE OF JUDAH". Remember what Jacob said in Genesis 49?

"Judah is a lion's whelp or a young lion... the sceptre shall not depart from Judah nor a lawgiver from between his feet until Shiloh comes". The lion that Jacob spoke of was Jesus Christ Himself!

Now let's put this into context. Do you remember what the name Judah means? It means "praise". Jesus is titled "The Lion of the Tribe of Judah" in the book of Revelation. In essence, He is the Lion of the tribe of Praise. HALLELUJAH! THERE'S A LION IN YOUR PRAISE! Why do you think the enemy tries to block your praise so much? Why do you think the adversary tries to silence you? Because he's afraid of your praise. Every time you open your mouth to bless God, the Lion begins to roar. Ever notice how everything in the jungle quiver and scatter when the lion, the king of the jungle roars? That's the same thing that happens in the spiritual realm when we open our mouths and let our Lion, the King of Kings roar. Every demon tremble; the very foundations of hell quake; prison doors fly open; chains fall off; fetters are broken; conditions shift; burdens are lifted; seasons change.

I dare you right now, right where you are, in spite of what you might be facing, regardless of what conditions may be like, open your mouth and shout! Roar! UNLEASH THE LION IN YOUR PRAISE! HALLELUJAH!

I challenge you right now to confront
your condition, stare it in the face,
open your mouth and release a praise
and let the Lion of the Tribe of Judah
roar on your behalf!

Precious

Cargo

On Board

PRECIOUS CARGO ON BOARD

Revelation 4:11
Thou art worthy, O Lord, to receive glory and honour and power: for thou hast created all things, and for thy pleasure they are and were created.

The appendix, not the one found at the end of a book, the one in the human body, is a small pouch, ranging from two to twenty centimetres in length. It is usually located in the lower right area of the abdomen near the right hip bone. For years, it was believed by people in the medical society and everyone else for that matter, that this was just an outgrowth in the human anatomy which served no apparent purpose. What strengthened their belief was that removing the appendix due to an infection known as appendicitis, revealed no side effects whatsoever. They couldn't be more wrong. It has recently been put forth that the appendix is actually a store house or haven for good bacteria which aid in the recovery process after bouts of dysentery, cholera or other gastrointestinal illnesses - so small and seemingly insignificant and irrelevant, yet so vitally important and serving so great a purpose.

In Revelation chapter four verse eleven, John related to us what he saw and heard in Heaven. In this particular passage, he made mention of the twenty four elders who fell prostrate before God and worshipped. The verbal expression of their adoration ascribed authorship to the rightful author of creation and echoes the intent of His heart for creation. "You are worthy Lord to receive glory, honour and power because You are the one who created all things and You created them for Your pleasure." In the Greek, which is the language of origin, the word rendered for "pleasure" is the word "thélēma", which translates to "purpose; determination; inclination; what one wishes or has determined shall be done". In effect, the twenty four elders were proclaiming that God created all things and every created thing carries a purpose. Every created thing, including you, yes you, is encoded with purpose. You were given life for a reason. The Creator had a determined end in mind when He fashioned you and gave you life. There is a specific assignment for your existence.

One of the greatest points of frustration for the billions of people occupying our planet today is that they don't know what their purpose is. It becomes even more complex having so many different things competing for your attention; so many questions needing your answer; so many problems jousting for your solution. How does one know beyond any doubt what it is that he is called to fulfil in the earth? It begins by knowing who you are. Who did the elders in heaven ascribe the authorship of creation to? To the Lord! He created all things. The word "created" is derived from the Greek word "ktízō" meaning to fabricate; found; form originally, through the idea of proprietorship of the manufacturer. You are God's original design; not a duplicate; not a knock off; not fake. You are an original. You are not a science experiment flung together in somebody's basement somewhere; neither were you put together in a factory in the middle of nowhere from scraps salvaged from the remains of other people. You were conceived in the mind of God and carefully and strategically placed in the earth at a time and place where the gifts, talents and abilities programmed into you will have the greatest impact on your environment and on the lives of those around you.

Having a misguided concept of who you are and why you exist will lead to abuse. Abuse is the improper or abnormal use of a thing; to use something contrary to its intended purpose. The word is derived from a Latin verb which is a compound word: "ab" which means "away or wrongly" and "uti" which means "to use". We can therefore safely conclude that whatever we do with our lives outside of what our Manufacturer intended, is improper use; it is self-abuse. A fitting example is the coca plant which first came into use, in recorded history, by the Incas who lived in the Andes. These Indians would chew the leaves of the plant which would speed up their breathing and cause their hearts to race. This was their remedy to counter the effects of altitude sickness which was common place due to the thin mountain air and the height at which they made their dwelling. By the 1800s, the plant was used in the enforcement of forced labour upon the Indians. Somewhere around 1532, scientists were able to extract a medicinal substance from the coca leaves, which came to be known as cocaine. This drug was being used in the treatment of a variety of ailments. Not long after, it became the subject of abuse to the point where, in one year, there was a report of approximately five thousand cocaine related deaths, not to mention the massive criminal enterprise which thrived from its misuse. Anyone who has ever visited the dentist to extract a tooth can attest to the usefulness of the drug. Yet the devastating evidence of its abuse due to its addictive properties is present everywhere. Where abuse exists, chaos is inevitable. Much of the world's chaos can be attributed to the widespread practice of people trying to answer questions they weren't born to answer or solve problems they aren't gifted to solve; in the meantime, the questions they are supposed to answer and the problems they are supposed to solve are either neglected or are being attempted by somebody else who was not placed on the world to touch them. Either way, chaos prevails.

So who are you really, at your core? David did a self-appraisal to find out this very thing and furnished us with the results in Psalm 139.

> *Psalms 139:14-16*
> *14 I will praise thee; for I am fearfully and wonderfully made: marvellous are thy works; and that my soul knoweth right well.*
> *15 My substance was not hid from thee, when I was made in secret, and curiously wrought in the lowest parts of the earth.*
> *16 Thine eyes did see my substance, yet being unperfect; and in thy book all my members were written, which in continuance were fashioned, when as yet there was none of them.*

Given that this was during the Old Testament era, then we go to the Hebrew language to understand more fully, what the psalmist was proclaiming to us. There are three words in verse fourteen which capture the attention: fearfully, wonderfully and marvellous. Fearfully comes from the Hebrew "yârê" which means to fear; revere; stand in awe of; honour; reverence; respect. You were created to be respected; to be reverenced. Not to be the object of ridicule. The highest of the highest among men should hold you in high regard. The mention of your name should warrant honour from every earth faring creature.

The words "wonderfully" and "marvellous" are derived from the same Hebrew root "pâlâ" which means distinct; distinguished; separate; set apart; extraordinary; to be difficult to understand. Among the billions of people occupying the earth today and the billions who have already transitioned, there cannot be found another one that is exactly like you. No one else had, have or will ever have the same fingerprints or DNA that you have. You are uniquely distinct. The creator did not look on someone else to get an idea of how to form you. You are not someone else's body double. You are a divine one of a kind - a designer's original. You are like a rare, hand crafted work of art, not to be compared with costume jewellery or fallalery, junk jewellery or fake jewellery as they are also known, which is nothing but pewter or brass plated with gold or silver, embellished with cheap and common rhinestone or cubic zirconia. The finished work of some are certainly eye catching with a touch of elegance, until after about two wears, then the colour begins to change, the cheap metals begin to rust and the embellishments begin to disappear one by one. No, no, no my friend. So uniquely extraordinary you are, that, in comparison, you would be like Queen Elizabeth's royal crown, made of gold, silver and platinum, decorated with two thousand eight hundred and sixty eight diamonds, two hundred and seventy three pearls, seventeen sapphires, eleven emeralds and five rubies including the famed Black Prince's Ruby, the three hundred and seventeen carat Cullinan II diamond also known as the Second Star of Africa and the one hundred and four carat Stuart Sapphire. You are indeed set apart. There's none else to compare you with.

In verse fifteen, the kingly worshipper speaks of being made in secret. The word secret comes from the Hebrew word "çêther" which means covering; shelter; hiding place. When God designed you, formulated your nature and character, encoded your gifts and abilities into you and determined your purpose, no one else was privy to what He was doing. You were sheltered from the eyes of men. No one saw what was put in you therefore no one knows who you are truly destined to be. This is why you can't live your life based on other people's opinion of you. David was perfectly qualified to draw this conclusion. His own family couldn't see beyond him being a shepherd. He wasn't even deemed fit to be considered for kingship but remember that God does not see as man sees, because man looks at the outward appearance but God looks on the heart. He knew that He had pre-programmed David to become king. Neither people's thoughts and opinions nor his present status were not decisive factors in this matter. As a matter of fact God used his present condition to propel him to his place of destiny. He was a shepherd. Being in the wilderness with the sheep prepared him for the call that was on his life. He had to defend the sheep against lions and bears. This taught him warfare and prepared him to deal with Goliath. He had enough time while he was in the green pastures and beside the still waters, to develop his skills in playing the harp. This positioned him to be summoned by Saul to the palace to play when the need arose. He had to lead the sheep. This prepared him to be a leader of the people of God. It's time to hold your head up. Snap out of despair. Stop viewing your present condition as a prison, withholding you from the purpose that keeps tugging at your spirit. What you are enduring right now is not a prison; rather, it is the place of preparation that will propel you to your place of purpose.

As the psalmist's enlightenment expanded, he came to the knowledge that not only was he made in secret but he was also curiously wrought in the lowest parts of the earth. The term "curiously wrought" is the English translation of the Hebrew word "râqam" which means variegated; embroider; needlework. What was in the mind of God when he envisioned you and breathed life into you, was not a bland, drab, insipid course of time from birth to death. You were designed to be a tapestry to display the awesome splendour and majesty of the creator. Your life was embroidered to testify of the glory of God. Notice how an embroiderer works. The threaded needle goes into the material and comes back out again, each stitch creating a loop or chain. The finished work displays a beautiful design, bursting with colour. The embroiderer is God. The material is your life. The threaded needle represents the struggles and the ups and downs that you experience. But the struggles and the ups and downs do not last forever; there's always a breakthrough. The Embroiderer allows them to enter and ensures that they come out again. You can't understand the reason for the needles entering your life until you see the finished product, how God, the Master Needleworker allows all things to work together for your good.

"Thine eyes did see my substance, yet being unperfect..." The author uses the Hebrew word "gôlem" which in the English language means "foetus". Know this you purpose carrier: there is nothing about you that is a surprise to God. You might have been a surprise to your parents; there are some things about your life that might be a surprise to other folks; there are things about your own life that might even be a surprise to you. But nothing about your life is a surprise to God. David declares that God's eyes were on him from the time he was a foetus, not yet developed... just a floating mass within his mother's womb. He spoke of how God had detailed his life in His book even before there was anything tangible to behold (and in Thy book all my members were written even before there was any of them). Isaiah captures this perfectly in chapter forty six of his book:

Isaiah 46:9-10
9 Remember the former things of old: for I am
God, and there is none else; I am God, and there is
none like me,

10 Declaring the end from the beginning, and from
ancient times the things that are not yet done,
saying, My counsel shall stand, and I will do all my
pleasure

There is indeed no one else like God who is able to declare the end from the beginning - to determine how a thing will end even before it begins. Let no one cause you to feel as if you were an accident; as if you crash landed into life with no purpose. You are a product of God's careful planning and orchestration. You have a cause in this world. Every builder works from a blueprint. The blueprint is not drawn while the building is being constructed. It is done before construction begins so that the builder can know the layout and dimensions of the building. The blueprint for your life was drawn before you came into this world.

Now, what the psalmist records next in verse seventeen, polishes the previous three verses and gives them the perfect sheen.

Psalms 139:17
How precious also are thy thoughts unto me, O God!
how great is the sum of them!

The word "precious" is from the Hebrew word "yâqar" which means prized; costly; highly valued; heavy. The word "thoughts" is from the Hebrew word "rêa" which goes beyond more than just an association of ideas. It means purpose; aim. The aim and purpose of God for your life is heavy. It is of high value; it is costly. You are carrying precious cargo. The mistake people make ever so often is to judge you based on what the outside of your vessel looks like. It's not the outer condition of the vessel that matters; it's the value of the cargo that it carries.

Okay then, so now that you have come to terms with who you are - who you really are, what next? Identify what kind of cargo you are carrying. Your cargo is the gifts, talents and abilities pre-programmed into you by God. What questions are your gifts suited to answer? What problems are they supposed to solve? Finding the answer to this does not require a two year sabbatical or an expedition around the world. It requires one simple step: ask your manufacturer. Who best can point you to your destiny but the one who gave you your destiny in the first place? Now don't get me wrong. It will require some effort on your part. You have to now be overly attentive, sharp, alert. You have to listen keenly for His directions because when you begin to ask, He will begin to answer, and He will respond in the way that He knows you will best hear and trust His voice. It could be through your dreams, through visions, through scripture. He could send someone with a word to you or perhaps through some sign in nature. But ensure that you don't make a mad rush at the first voice you hear or the first sign you see. Be patient; wait for confirmation. When God speaks, He will confirm it.

Then comes the preparation process. One of the greatest errors that has killed some of the greatest visions and has caused some potentially great men to fail miserably is the act of stepping out prematurely into a venture. The human nature always wants to see everything now, all at once. Everything must be instant. While in some cases it might be convenient, as far as the vision and call on your life is concerned, instant is detrimental. Preparation is necessary. The word "prepare" means to make ready beforehand for some activity, purpose or use. It is a Latin compound word. "Pre" means "before" and "pare" means "to cut or trim off the excess or unnecessary portions." The preparation process is where you trim away negative habits and tendencies that will only work against you when you step out into the vision. It is the place where you cut off toxic relationships. This is where we get drastic because sometimes some of those toxic relationships are relatives or people who are dear to us. But you have to make that all important decision... are you willing to sit with people who are going nowhere and end up nowhere with them or is the call on your life so great that you're willing to give up your seat on the fast flight to nowhere, bid the passengers goodbye and step out into the vision?

Think about it... an Olympic champion athlete doesn't become a champion overnight. The media provides us with the coverage of the ten seconds or less from the one hundred metre starting blocks to the finish line and the glitz and glamour that follow. What we rarely see are the weeks, months and years of preparation, which is the literal cutting away of excess pounds as that runner transforms his body into an indomitable running machine. He also trims away at other areas of his life, being careful of what he eats or ingests, making the tough decision to give up certain foods and drinks that may contain substances that are against regulations. A majority of the time he would normally spend just unwinding or relaxing has to now be concentrated on whipping his body into shape and developing his technique. These are painstaking decisions that he makes because, to him, the call is greater than the comforts.

The preparation process is not just the time of cutting away. It is also the time of gaining. During this time we gain the wisdom, the knowledge, the confidence, the will power, the drive, the passion, the connections and relationships that will be necessary not just for gaining success, but for gaining success with excellence and maintaining it. There will always be something that we need to learn no matter how learned we consider ourselves to be. We also need the wisdom to know how to apply the knowledge we gain. Confidence is necessary for those times when dream killers and vision assassins show up... and trust me, they will show up. Sometimes they come in the form of leaders; people that we look up to and trust, withholding vital information or deliberately shutting some doors in your face. Sometimes they come in the form of family members, relatives and friends who discourage you, telling you that what you're trying to do will not work and even offering "a better option". Oftentimes they genuinely believe that they are helping you... involuntary assassins they are indeed. Sometimes they appear in the form of banks and other financial institutions who withhold much needed resources because, in their opinion, it won't work. What do you do in those times when the killers and assassins come? Do you roll over and play dead. No! Step out of their circle and forge new connections and relationships with people who are of like mind as you are; people who believe in your vision and have a genuine heart to see the success of it. Understand also, that no matter how confident you are in yourself, you can't do it alone. A true God given vision is always bigger than the visionary. You will need other people and their gifts to bring yours to success. Then there will be those times when you feel like calling it quits. You begin to think long and hard until you begin to convince your own mind that what you are attempting is just plain foolish, especially if it's something that no one else ever did before. There might be times when it seems as if everything is at a standstill and you start to believe that it's the end. This is when will power becomes necessary; the drive and the passion to push ahead even when pushing ahead doesn't seem to make sense.

The preparation process is also the place where you develop your mission statement; that watchword that will guide you as you move towards your destiny. It is where you write the vision and make it plain; document your plan in a detailed manner. Why is this necessary? Remember, you alone can't do it. You need other folks with their resources, gifts, abilities and energy. You might have the plan laid out in your mind but the people you need to help you are not mind readers. When you carefully document the vision you have in your mind then they can run with you as you run with it.

So what do you do after the preparation process? Just get up and do it! Get practical. You've already done the ground work. The foundation is set. Stir up the faith within you and begin fulfilling what you have spent all that time preparing for. Remember, you are carrying precious cargo. A cargo ship was not designed and built to remain in the docks. Its purpose is to deliver goods from one point to another. It takes its cargo from the point of supply to the point of need. There is a problem somewhere waiting for the solution you possess; there is a question that's waiting for the answer you are carrying. Move to your destination and offload what the All Wise God has laden you with. YOU HAVE PRECIOUS CARGO ON BOARD!

You're Carrying Precious Cargo!

It's time to leave the docks; set sail
to your God-ordained destination and
offload the precious cargo you have within
you. Someone is waiting for the solution
you possess and for the answer you are
carrying.

Behold I Give
Unto You
Power

BEHOLD
I GIVE UNTO YOU POWER

The Gospel of Luke paints a vivid picture of the life of Jesus. The book was written as a letter addressed to one known as Theophilus, providing a detailed account of the life and works of Jesus.

> *Luke 1:3*
> *It seemed good to me also, having had perfect understanding of all things from the very first, to write unto thee in order, most excellent Theophilus.*

Not much is known of the recipient. His name means "friend of God". He is believed to be a gentile of high rank as seen from the greeting of Luke: "most excellent". But the emphasis is not on the recipient of the letter, it's on the person who is the subject of the letter, Jesus Christ.

In the ninth chapter of the book, Luke records that Jesus sent out His twelve disciples, endowing them with authority to enter the cities, preaching the Gospel of the Kingdom of God with the power to heal the sick, cure diseases, cast out demons and demonstrate the awesomeness of God's Kingdom.

> *Luke 9:1-2*
> *1 Then he called his twelve disciples together, and gave them power and authority over all devils, and to cure diseases.*
> *2 And he sent them to preach the kingdom of God, and to heal the sick.*

In the tenth chapter, Luke states that Jesus appointed another seventy, separate and apart from the twelve that were sent out in the previous chapter. Who were these seventy? Where did they come from? What we need to bear in mind is that even though the Gospels focus mainly on twelve disciples, Jesus had a multitude of followers who were committed to His teachings. In chapter nine He sends out the twelve; in chapter ten he sends out seventy more. This is how I like to look at it: the twelve were the ministers and the seventy were the congregation.

> *Luke 10:1*
> *After these things the Lord appointed other seventy also, and sent them two and two before his face into every city and place, whither he himself would come.*

As you read on you realise that the same directive, the same mandate and the same authority He gave to the twelve, He also gave to the seventy. Whatever was issued to the ministers was also issued to the congregation. The anointing was the same; the miraculous power was the same. It's no surprise then that the results were also the same. The sick were healed, the lame walked, blinded eyes were opened and demons were cast out. There are so many congregations in which people are shackled under the belief that the gifts, anointing and operations of the Spirit of God are only for those appointed to particular offices; as if the power of the Holy Spirit is reserved for the bishops and pastors and evangelists and prophets. Hear what Paul says:

> *1 Corinthians 12:1*
> *Now concerning spiritual gifts, brethren, I would not have you ignorant.*

> *1 Corinthians 12:4-11*
> *4 Now there are diversities of gifts, but the same Spirit.*
> *5 And there are differences of administrations, but the same Lord.*
> *6 And there are diversities of operations, but it is the same God which worketh all in all.*
> *7 But the manifestation of the Spirit is given to every man to profit withal.*
> *8 For to one is given by the Spirit the word of wisdom; to another the word of knowledge by the same Spirit;*
> *9 To another faith by the same Spirit; to another the gifts of healing by the same Spirit;*
> *10 To another the working of miracles; to another prophecy; to another discerning of spirits; to*

> *another divers kinds of tongues; to another the interpretation of tongues:*
> *11 But all these worketh that one and the selfsame Spirit, dividing to every man severally as he will.*

The apostle starts out by addressing the misconceptions in the church surrounding the gifts of the Spirit: "I do not want you to be ignorant". He then proceeds to show the Corinthians that even though there are different gifts, they all come from and through the Holy Spirit. There are different offices but all of them come from God. The gifts may operate and manifest in different ways but it is God Himself that works through them. The man of God then highlights the various spiritual gifts and look what he says in verse eleven: "the Holy Spirit distributes the gifts to EVERY MAN according to HIS WILL". Wow! This is amazing. "Every man" doesn't mean those holding titles and offices in the church. "Every man" means every single believer in the Body of Christ. And it is not your church leaders who determine what gifts you operate in; it's the Holy Spirit who makes that determination. Every believer is gifted and can see the power of God manifest through the operation of the gift or gifts within them. The sad truth is that sometimes some folks are muzzled and even ostracised when they begin to flow in their God-given gift just because the leaders or the holders of offices might not see that same gift manifesting through themselves.

Now let's continue with Luke's account. The seventy went out, did what they were mandated by Jesus to do and returned.

> *Luke 10:17*
> *And the seventy returned again with joy, saying, Lord, even the devils are subject unto us through thy name.*

What a glorious return. It was like an army going out to battle against a formidable foe and returning in triumph. They returned with joy exclaiming that even the devils were subjected to them through the name of Jesus. The Greek word used for the word "subject" is the word "hypotásso". Now this word can be used in two contexts. Firstly, it is used as a military term. In this sense it means to arrange a troop or a division of soldiers in military fashion under the command of a general. We know that when a general issues a command, the troop has to fall in line in strict obedience or else there will be consequences. What were they saying? "Every time we encountered a demon, all we had to do was stand in the authority you gave us, issue the command and whatever we commanded, that devil had to move in obedience". Remember Jesus' encounter with the man possessed with a legion of devils at Gadarenes? Without resisting or questioning His authority, they obeyed the command of the General, Jesus Christ.

Secondly, the word is used in non-military sense and when used in this context it means "to voluntarily give in, assume responsibility, cooperate and carry a burden". What does this mean for us as believers? Understand that sicknesses, diseases, burdens, negative cycles, curses and the various hardships of life that plague people are not manufactured or distributed by God. They are products of the devil and his hosts. Whatever it is that afflicts you, plagues you and works against your purpose, destiny and welfare is instigated by the devil, not by God and there are demonic entities working in the background to ensure that these afflictions take full effect. But we have been given such a level of authority as ambassadors for Christ, that wherever we see the manifestation of these afflictions, we can command the devils working behind them to voluntarily give in or to surrender, to assume responsibility for the affliction they have brought, to cooperate with and not oppose our command and to take the burden or affliction and carry it themselves. For example, you encounter someone suffering with cancer. Now, you know the individual is suffering and it's not of God. You know that that's a sickness, which is not of God. In the name of Jesus, command the devil causing the affliction of cancer upon that individual to surrender, take responsibility for the affliction, remove the burden from that person's life and carry it himself. This, my friend, is deliverance. Can you see the picture now child of God? You are no ordinary person. You are beyond ordinary, above average. Devils are subject to you!

Now, to understand how the devils are brought under subjection to us, we must take the last phrase of their statement into consideration: "through Thy name". When we ask a person what their name is, the automatic response is to give us the label that was given to them by their parents at birth to identify them. That's just what a name is to us. But when we examine this from Biblical perspective, we see that a name goes far beyond one's identifying label. The name actually defined the nature and character of the individual. From the Greek, the word rendered is "ónoma" which, when translated to English, encompasses ones rank, authority, essence, character and nature. Take Jacob for instance. The Hebrew name meant "supplanter or heel-catcher". He was so named because during birth he grabbed on to his twin brother's heel:

> *Genesis 25:21-26*
> *21 And Isaac intreated the LORD for his wife, because she was barren: and the LORD was intreated of him, and Rebekah his wife conceived.*
> *22 And the children struggled together within her; and she said, If it be so, why am I thus? And she went to enquire of the LORD.*
> *23 And the LORD said unto her, Two nations are in thy womb, and two manner of people shall be separated from thy bowels; and the one people shall*

be stronger than the other people; and the elder shall serve the younger.

24 And when her days to be delivered were fulfilled, behold, there were twins in her womb.

25 And the first came out red, all over like an hairy garment; and they called his name Esau.

26 And after that came his brother out, and his hand took hold on Esau's heel; and his name was called Jacob: and Isaac was threescore years old when she bare them.

Throughout the course of his life he portrayed the essence of his name, robbing his brother of his birthright and his blessing through trickery and deceit:

Genesis 27:30-36

30 And it came to pass, as soon as Isaac had made an end of blessing Jacob, and Jacob was yet scarce gone out from the presence of Isaac his father, that Esau his brother came in from his hunting.

31 And he also had made savoury meat, and brought it unto his father, and said unto his father, Let my father arise, and eat of his son's venison, that thy soul may bless me.

32 And Isaac his father said unto him, Who art thou? And he said, I am thy son, thy firstborn Esau.

33 And Isaac trembled very exceedingly, and said, Who? where is he that hath taken venison, and brought it me, and I have eaten of all before thou camest, and have blessed him? yea, and he shall be blessed.

34 And when Esau heard the words of his father, he cried with a great and exceeding bitter cry, and said unto his father, Bless me, even me also, O my father.

35 And he said, Thy brother came with subtilty, and hath taken away thy blessing.

36 And he said, Is not he rightly named Jacob? for he hath supplanted me these two times: he took away my birthright; and, behold, now he hath taken away my blessing. And he said, Hast thou not reserved a blessing for me?

And even while at Laban's house, suffering the plight of harsh work conditions and unfair wage negotiations, Jacob managed to prosper still:

Genesis 30:25-43

25 And it came to pass, when Rachel had born Joseph, that Jacob said unto Laban, Send me away, that I may go unto mine own place, and to my country.

26 Give me my wives and my children, for whom I have served thee, and let me go: for thou knowest my service which I have done thee.

27 And Laban said unto him, I pray thee, if I have found favour in thine eyes, tarry: for I have learned by experience that the LORD hath blessed me for thy sake.

28 And he said, Appoint me thy wages, and I will give it.

29 And he said unto him, Thou knowest how I have served thee, and how thy cattle was with me.

30 For it was little which thou hadst before I came, and it is now increased unto a multitude; and the LORD hath blessed thee since my coming: and now when shall I provide for mine own house also?

31 And he said, What shall I give thee? And Jacob said, Thou shalt not give me any thing: if thou wilt do this thing for me, I will again feed and keep thy flock:

32 I will pass through all thy flock to day, removing from thence all the speckled and spotted cattle, and all the brown cattle among the sheep, and the spotted and speckled among the goats: and of such shall be my hire.

33 So shall my righteousness answer for me in time to come, when it shall come for my hire before thy face: every one that is not speckled and spotted among the goats, and brown among the sheep, that shall be counted stolen with me.

34 And Laban said, Behold, I would it might be according to thy word.

35 And he removed that day the he goats that were ringstraked and spotted, and all the she goats that were speckled and spotted, and every one that had some white in it, and all the brown among the sheep, and gave them into the hand of his sons.

36 And he set three days' journey betwixt himself and Jacob: and Jacob fed the rest of Laban's flocks.

37 And Jacob took him rods of green poplar, and of the hazel and chesnut tree; and pilled white strakes in them, and made the white appear which was in the rods.

38 And he set the rods which he had pilled before the flocks in the gutters in the watering troughs when the flocks came to drink, that they should conceive when they came to drink.

39 And the flocks conceived before the rods, and brought forth cattle ringstraked, speckled, and spotted.

40 And Jacob did separate the lambs, and set the faces of the flocks toward the ringstraked, and all the brown in the flock of Laban; and he put his own flocks by themselves, and put them not unto Laban's cattle.

41 And it came to pass, whensoever the stronger cattle did conceive, that Jacob laid the rods before the eyes of the cattle in the gutters, that they might conceive among the rods.

42 But when the cattle were feeble, he put them not in: so the feebler were Laban's, and the stronger Jacob's.

43 And the man increased exceedingly, and had much cattle, and maidservants, and menservants, and camels, and asses.

There are numerous instances throughout the scriptures of how one's name was identical to his nature and character, but you get the picture. Now, when the seventy returned and declared that "the devils are subject to us through Thy name", it was not simply a matter of saying "in the name of Jesus", rather, it was a matter of acting in His authority and portraying His nature, essence and character while declaring His name. You see, demons are not afraid of the mere utterance of Jesus' name. What could possibly drive me to say something like that? Do you remember the account in the book of Acts with the seven sons of Sceva?

> *Acts 19:13-17*
>
> *13 Then certain of the vagabond Jews, exorcists, took upon them to call over them which had evil spirits the name of the Lord Jesus, saying, We adjure you by Jesus whom Paul preacheth.*
>
> *14 And there were seven sons of one Sceva, a Jew, and chief of the priests, which did so.*
>
> *15 And the evil spirit answered and said, Jesus I know, and Paul I know; but who are ye?*
>
> *16 And the man in whom the evil spirit was leaped on them, and overcame them, and prevailed against them, so that they fled out of that house naked and wounded.*
>
> *17 And this was known to all the Jews and Greeks also dwelling at Ephesus; and fear fell on them all, and the name of the Lord Jesus was magnified.*

The first thing that jumps out is that the Jews mentioned here were using the name of Jesus but they did not even know Jesus for themselves... *"In the name of Jesus whom Paul preacheth"*. Remember what I said? Demons are not afraid of the mere utterance of the name of Jesus. Look at verse fifteen above. The evil spirit which possessed the individual upon whom this laughable example of exorcism was being performed, started to speak through the man... "Jesus I know". What? The demon said "Jesus!" Now let's reason. If demons were afraid of the mere mention of the name, would they be uttering the name themselves? I think not! What they are afraid of; what causes them to tremble; what delivers a crushing blow to their operations is when the believer uses the name of Jesus while standing in the authority of the name and his or her life bears the likeness of Jesus' nature, character and essence.

Jesus, in responding to the seventy as they gave excited report of what they witnessed and experienced in fulfilling their mandate, declared "I beheld Satan as lightning fall from heaven".

> *Luke 10:18*
> *And he said unto them, I beheld Satan as lightning fall from heaven.*

Wow! As these humble ambassadors went out representing Christ, the satanic forces that expressed influence for so long over the various cities, were dealt an unexpected, swift and decisive blow. Satan, the prince of the power of the air; commander in chief over principalities, powers, the rulers of the darkness of this world and spiritual wickedness in high places, fell from heaven like lightning. When lightning strikes it is both extremely swift and clearly visible. So was the fall of the accuser of the brethren. When we stand in the name of Jesus, tell me who can stand before us!

Then Jesus makes a grand deposit to the seventy, which, by extension, was also made to us who believe in His name and represent Him in the advancement of His Kingdom here on earth.

> *Luke 10:19*
> *Behold, I give unto you power to tread on serpents and scorpions, and over all the power of the enemy: and nothing shall by any means hurt you.*

Let's dissect this verse and see the vast revelatory wealth it holds. The word "give" as used in the verse comes from the Greek "dídōmi", which has a very wide application. It means to give freely or bestow gifts of one's own accord; to hand over something with the intent of it being administered; to restore to someone who had ownership before. What was it that Christ gave? Power! This means firstly, that the power was given freely. Secondly, it was His intent that the power should be administered or put to use by the recipient, not to be stored up or laid down to gather dust. Thirdly, it was restored, given back to who owned it before. You mean we owned the power before? Oh yes, we did!

> *Genesis 1:26-28*
> *26 And God said, Let us make man in our image, after our likeness: and let them have dominion over*

> *the fish of the sea, and over the fowl of the air, and over the cattle, and over all the earth, and over every creeping thing that creepeth upon the earth.*
> *27 So God created man in his own image, in the image of God created he him; male and female created he them.*
> *28 And God blessed them, and God said unto them, Be fruitful, and multiply, and replenish the earth, and subdue it: and have dominion over the fish of the sea, and over the fowl of the air, and over every living thing that moveth upon the earth.*

See that word "dominion" in the passage above? That's the power to subdue, to dominate, to walk in authority. It was bestowed upon man at the time of creation. Mankind lost it due to sin but Christ came and restored it. Our dominion has been restored; authority has been transferred back to us for us to administer it.

"Behold I give unto you power." We see the word "power" used in that verse two times but to grasp the full understanding, we have to go back to the language of origin. The word "power" is indeed used twice but they originate from two separate Greek words and therefore have two completely different meanings. The first occurrence as uttered by Jesus is in reference to the believers: "I give unto you (the children of God; the ones called by my name; the ones authorised to act on my behalf) power". In this instance the Greek word is "exousía" which means authority; governmental influence; the power of him whose will and commands must be submitted to by others and obeyed; jurisdiction or judicial authority (the kind of authority the judge has in a courtroom). Wow! Look at the level of authority the King has released to us. This was not meant for a select few, this was meant for the Body of Christ. Yet so many of us run around like weaklings, whimpering in fear at every threat the enemy breathes out. We have judicial power. The world is our courtroom. In the name of Jesus we have the legal right to pass sentence on every devil from the pit of hell operating illegally in the earth realm. A judge doesn't cloak his face in his judicial garb when sentencing a criminal. He doesn't hide behind the bailiff. He issues the sentence with the authority vested in him, bangs his gavel, closes the case and returns to his chamber. That's how we are expected to operate. We have the authority.

The next occurrence of the word "power" is in reference to the adversary: "over all the power of the enemy". The Greek word rendered is "dunamis" which translates to dynamic force; ability; the power residing in one by virtue of his nature. Now let's apply some deductive reasoning. The Word of God declares that Jesus has spoiled principalities and powers...

> *Colossians 2:15*
> *And having spoiled principalities and powers, he made a shew of them openly, triumphing over them in it.*

The word "spoil" is derived from the Greek "apekdyomai" which means to despoil (to severely damage or ruin; to forcefully take what is valuable; to strip of belongings, possessions or value) and to disarm (to take weapons from; to render harmless; to deprive of means, reason or disposition to be hostile). The devil's arsenal has been emptied of all dynamic force. He has been rendered powerless. He has been stripped naked of all authority which means the only thing he is left with is ability. He doesn't have the power to kill you. He only has the ability to present death before you. It can't do you anything unless you come into agreement with it and give it legal grounds to take effect. He doesn't have the power to cause you to sin. He only has the ability to tempt you with sin. You have the authority to stand in victory, resist him, rebuke him and be triumphant.

Our authority permits us to tread upon serpents and scorpions and to put all the enemy's ability and efforts under our feet. The Greek word for "tread" is "patéō" which means to trample, crush with the feet; to advance by setting foot upon; to successfully encounter the greatest perils..." Why then do we fear? Why do we cause worry to take hold of us? The place for perils and problems is not up in our faces, it's under our feet. The very things designed to thwart your destiny, your future, your prosperity, your blessing, are not above you. They are designed by the devil but positioned by

God to be your stepping stones to your place of greatness. Those serpents (regarded as a type of sly cunning and figuratively represents artful, malicious people who spend their energy to thwart your efforts, demean your character and sabotage your opportunities) and scorpions (figurative of those who sting and pierce by their evil deeds and by releasing curses and speaking negative words against you in an attempt to poison your life) are under your feet! Those are the dangers that lurk in the valley of the shadow of death, but as the psalmist declares, so we likewise declare: "we shall fear no evil".

Jesus closed the verse with a most powerful declaration: "and nothing shall by any means hurt you". What a blessed assurance. The word "hurt" in the Greek is "adikéō" which means to act unjustly or wickedly; to be criminal; to violate the law in some way. Nothing shall violate the laws that govern your life. Not the laws of earth. Remember that as a child of God, you are in the world but not of the world. The laws of the Kingdom of God supersede the laws of the world you live in. When the enemy and his diabolic criminal enterprise seek to bring sickness against you, the laws of the Kingdom of God state that with His stripes you are healed. When there is pronouncement of death, the law states that you shall not die but live to declare the works of the Lord. When forces form alliances against you the law states that a thousand shall fall at your side and ten thousand at your right hand but it shall not come near you. When lack and poverty seek to get a foot hold, the law declares that you are blessed in the city, blessed in the field, blessed going out and coming in. When sadness and sorrow draw near, the law declares that the joy of the Lord is your strength. When rejection props up its ugly head, the law pronounces that though mother and father forsake you, the Lord will take you up. No matter what the general of evil brings against you, the laws will not be violated by any means. Nothing shall by any means harm you!

The Power

Of

Agreement

THE POWER OF AGREEMENT

Several years ago I was a teacher at a preparatory school; a job that I held for eleven years. My memory jogs back to one particular year when our first daughter, the only child we had at the time, was about to begin second grade, or, as we say it in Jamaica, "grade two". The summer holidays were drawing to a close and everyone seemed to be feverishly making back to school preparations for their children... everyone except us. We had less than one week to go and no money whatsoever to secure the necessaries. All we had up to that point was a pack of notebooks (not even the ones required for her class) and a few erasers which she had left over from grade one. We had not been able to purchase her text books, uniforms, shoes, bag... nothing. I remember just before we went to sleep the Tuesday night, my wife and I were speaking about the situation. We came into agreement and our final conclusion on the matter was that five days is enough time for God to do a miracle. We did not know how it would come or where it would come from but we were in agreement and expectation.

I woke up the Wednesday morning preparing to attend a staff meeting at the school where I worked. The meeting was scheduled for ten o'clock but I was trying to leave out early enough to get some other business sorted out before the meeting time. As I was almost ready, my phone rang. I was wondering if I should answer now or call back later because answering the call at that time could delay me and throw off my timing. I answered. On the other end of the line was a church sister, a woman of God that we were acquainted with. The first thing she asked was, "how are you?" My reply, "all is well", speaking by faith and calling those things which are not as though they were. If my memory serves me correctly, the conversation went on for twenty six minutes. At the end of the call, she asked "by the way, how is Brianna doing for back to school?" Now this question was more direct. I had to be straight up. I said "sister, we haven't gotten the things she needs but we just agreed last night that five days is enough time for God to do a miracle". Before the words from my mouth could get cold, she blurted out "you don't have to wait for five days, I can be a part of the miracle now". Can you imagine? In just a matter of hours God did it, but, hold your horses there for one moment. This sister lived miles upon miles away. She didn't want to send it through the bank or through the remittance agency. She wanted me to collect it personally. Now, we had already determined that it couldn't be any more than five thousand Jamaican dollars, which really couldn't reach far, and to spend the fare to travel to where she was and back home just didn't seem to make sense. But that's the way it is when God is working out a breakthrough... it often doesn't make any sense during the process until you get to the end result.

After the staff meeting ended that afternoon, my wife, my daughter and I travelled all the way to the miracle's address; a journey which required two taxis and a bus. I know what you're thinking... "you said going there didn't seem to make sense but now you're going with the entire family". Well, we arrived sometime in the evening hours and sat on the veranda and chatted for a little while. She served us a delicious meal of curried chicken with yam, boiled dumpling and boiled banana and handed me a brown envelope. Because of the time, traveling back home that evening would have proven too taxing so we made a decision to spend the night there. The minute we got into the room where we would sleep, we tore the envelope open to find out the value of its contents. Hallelujah! It was two hundred US dollars! At that time that amount valued approximately twenty thousand Jamaican dollars. That was more than enough to cover Brianna's back to school expenses and to even be a blessing to someone else that was in need.

But that wasn't the full story. Neither was it the end of the story. The sister that God used to "be a part of the miracle" related her side of the transaction to us. She said that when she called me the morning, God had told her to call and ask the very question she asked at the end of the twenty six minutes conversation: "how is Brianna for back to school?" God had instructed her to bless us with the two hundred dollars. After she hung up, she started to wrestle with faith, telling God that she would give us half and keep the other half because that was what she needed for her daughter's back to school preparations. She said she could hear the voice of God explicitly saying "no, I told you to give them all, not half". She finally came to a place of faith where she decided to trust God and obey His instruction. As soon as she did so, her phone rang. It was an overseas call and the first thing the person on the other end of the line asked was "how is your daughter for back to school?" Amazing God! Oh the glory He releases and the blessings we receive when we walk in simple obedience. What favours we forfeit when we choose not to obey, sabotaging our own miracles in the process.

As we got ready to take the long journey back home, we decided to pay a visit to a friend of the family that lived a short distance from where we were. Upon saying farewell, one of the family members shook my hand leaving a crumpled piece of paper in my palm. Fifty Canadian dollars! Can I tell you friends, when we are down to nothing, God is always up to something. All our situations require sometimes is the power of agreement. When you can find someone of like spirit and like faith to agree with you in the name of Jesus, life and nature can do nothing but flow in harmony to bring about your breakthrough.

I love the way Jesus said it:

> *Matthew 18:19-20*
> *19 Again I say unto you, That if two of you shall agree on earth as touching anything that they shall ask, it shall be done for them of my Father which is in heaven.*
> *20 For where two or three are gathered together in my name, there am I in the midst of them.*

Now this is a powerful message. Agreement on earth in Jesus' name brings divine response from heaven.

The word "agree" in Greek is "symphōnéō", which gives a meaning of harmony; to stipulate by compact; to be in accord. It is where we get the word "symphony" from. A symphony is a long piece of music sometimes played in four parts, performed by an orchestra. There are different types of orchestras, but symphonies are played by symphony orchestras. These consist of over one hundred instruments from four families or sections of instruments: strings, brass, woodwind and percussion and playing under the directorship of a conductor; one man conducting hundreds and even thousands of players to play at the same tempo. His ears are so well trained that he can detect the slightest variation. He is a human metronome, keeping everyone in unison to produce a musical masterpiece. The World Record Academy records the largest symphony orchestra gathering on a football field in Frankfurt, Germany in 2016, consisting of seven thousand five hundred and forty eight musicians playing for forty five minutes, directed by Wolf Kerschek. Wow! Such a vast number, all playing in the same key, keeping the same rhythm to give birth to a melodic work of art. This is what agreement is and what it does. Agreement on earth produces a melody that moves Heaven to move on our behalf. Jesus Himself is the composer of our symphony with the Holy Spirit being our maestro, keeping our faith in harmony to bring about a divine purpose.

There is a barrage of instances in scripture which testifies of the power of agreement, beginning with the very first chapter of the very first book of the Bible.

> *Genesis 1:26*
> *And God said, Let us make man in our image, after our likeness: and let them have dominion over the fish of the sea, and over the fowl of the air, and over the cattle, and over all the earth, and over every creeping thing that creepeth upon the earth.*

God said "let US make man in OUR image, after OUR likeness." The words "us" and "our" signify a coming together to achieve a common purpose. The Godhead: The Father, The Word and The Spirit working in unison to complete creation by creating and mandating man to have dominion over every other created thing.

Again we see the power of agreement as we trek back to the time in Israel when Saul was king. The Israelites had been placed under such restriction by the Philistines that the only weapons of war they possessed were two swords, one belonging to King Saul and the other to his son Jonathan. They weren't even permitted to sharpen their own agricultural tools. They had to go into the towns of the Philistines for that. It's never acceptable to settle for mediocrity, becoming comfortable in rudimentary living; there has to come a time when you declare "enough is enough!" When you come to that point in time, one of the greatest and most useful pieces of advice is to find someone who can agree with you, being wise to know also that you cannot pull any and everyone into your conquest... choose carefully!

> *1 Samuel 14:1*
> *Now it came to pass upon a day, that Jonathan the son of Saul said unto the young man that bare his armour, Come, and let us go over to the Philistines' garrison, that is on the other side. But he told not his father.*

Notice that? Jonathan came in agreement with his armour bearer; one who remains nameless in scripture, yet, this was someone that Jonathan trusted with his life. He knew the spirit, nature and character of the man. He was assured that this was not someone that would call it quits and leave him in the heat of battle to face the enemy all by his lonesome. This was a man who was willing to stick with Jonathan in the face of certain death because the fulfilment of the mandate was greater to him than the preservation of his own life. Notice also the last sentence in the verse. He did not tell his father. Why? Because Jonathan knew that as much as his father was the king, he would not have seen the possibility that he was seeing. He would have envisioned defeat where Jonathan was seeing victory; he would have declared it impossible when Jonathan embraced the possibilities; he would have been an instrument of discouragement when Jonathan was impregnated with courage. I say it again, you can't come in agreement with any and everyone... choose carefully.

> *1 Samuel 14:6-7*
> *6 And Jonathan said to the young man that bare his armour, Come, and let us go over unto the garrison of these uncircumcised: it may be that the LORD will work for us: for there is no restraint to the LORD to save by many or by few.*

7 And his armourbearer said unto him, Do all that is in thine heart: turn thee; behold, I am with thee according to thy heart.

Jonathan was no doubt familiar with the mighty victories that God wrought on behalf of Israel in their conquest of the Promised Land. He perhaps recalled the account of Gideon leading an army of three hundred men into battle against an innumerable host and coming out victorious. Hear the voice of faith speaking through him: "there is no restraint to the Lord to save by many or by few", in other words, whether it be an army of one or one hundred thousand, victory is sure once God is the Commander In Chief.

The response of the armour bearer seals the agreement perfectly: "anything you decide to do, do it, I'm right there with you in any decision you make." Indeed, there can be no agreement if both parties do not actually agree. It's no agreement at all if one party is forced or bribed into it. Agreement must be consensual. It is in such atmospheres that the greatest victories are realised.

1 Samuel 14:13-14
13 And Jonathan climbed up upon his hands and upon his feet, and his armourbearer after him: and they fell before Jonathan; and his armourbearer slew after him.

> *14 And that first slaughter, which Jonathan and his armourbearer made, was about twenty men, within as it were an half acre of land, which a yoke of oxen might plow.*

The agreement was not just a verbal formality; there was a practical fulfilment of the terms. Two men, one sword, facing a battalion that far outnumbered them and was much more equipped for war than them. But as Jonathan took down the Philistine soldiers one by one, the armour bearer came behind him ensuring that as they fell, they would never be able to rise again. Through the mutual agreement of two, God served a massive blow to the Philistine regiment and restored hope and courage to a whimpering Israelite army.

Solomon, in his great reflection on life as recorded in the book of Ecclesiastes, sums up the benefits of agreement in four verses.

> *Ecclesiastes 4:9-12*
> *9 Two are better than one; because they have a good reward for their labour.*
> *10 For if they fall, the one will lift up his fellow: but woe to him that is alone when he falleth; for he hath not another to help him up.*
> *11 Again, if two lie together, then they have heat: but how can one be warm alone?*
> *12 And if one prevail against him, two shall withstand him; and a threefold cord is not quickly broken.*

In verse eleven, the wise king uses a sexual connotation to illustrate his lesson and that's very much expected from a man who had a harem of seven hundred wives and three hundred concubines. "If two lie together they have heat, but how can one be warm alone." In the Hebrew, the words "lie together" come from "shâkab" which means to be lain with sexually or to have a sexual connection. What happens when two persons come together in a sexual connection? They have heat. The word "heat" there is the Hebrew "châmam" meaning to become aroused or inflamed with passion. Such passion cannot be stirred by one individual all by himself, it is stirred in an atmosphere of agreement between two sexually consenting individuals. Rightly expressed by Solomon, how can a person be warm by himself or herself? The word "warm" as used in that particular context has nothing to do with temperature. It's Hebrew origin is "yâcham" which means to mate and to conceive (become pregnant). Agreement always produces. Individuals cannot mate or conceive by themselves, at least not according to God's order of things. But when individuals come together in an atmosphere of mutual agreement, production is set in motion and the platform is set to be fruitful, multiply and replenish.

Coming into agreement with others who can see what you see, believe as you believe and stand with the same level of determination and faith as you do will make the seemingly impossible exploits possible; such agreement makes the most arduous endeavours work out with ease. After the great deluge in Noah's days, when the earth began to be repopulated, the Bible declares in Genesis chapter eleven that they were all traveling together from the east and everyone spoke the same language. As they arrived at a a particular plain which was situated in Shinar, they forged an agreement. In order to keep mankind together, they were going to build a city with a tower which reached up to heaven which could house all the inhabitants of earth at that particular time. Brick by brick they began erecting this massive edifice.

> *Genesis 11:5-6*
> *5 And the LORD came down to see the city and the tower, which the children of men builded.*
> *6 And the LORD said, Behold, the people is one, and they have all one language; and this they begin to do: and now nothing will be restrained from them, which they have imagined to do.*

As God observed the progress of the people He noted that their progress was as a result of their agreement and the unity that they had through having a common vision, hoping for and working toward the same end and speaking the same language. My friend, I implore you to find others that speak the same faith language as you. Lock your faith with them and begin working toward a common purpose. I declare to you that in so doing, nothing shall be restrained from you. What miracle have you been praying for? What breakthrough have you been expecting? What promise of God has seemingly been hijacked by the enemy? I rehearse for you the assurance of Jesus, that if any two on earth shall agree, any two... they don't have to be ranked on the same level socially; they don't have to be from the same culture; they don't have to share the same parental background or financial standing. They just need to envision the same end and speak the same language of faith. The end result will be that our Father in Heaven will grant the objective of the agreement.

Nature gives one of the greatest testimonies of the power of agreement. There is a particular type of tree called tabonuco, found only in specific countries. These trees are characterised by their height; towering above all the other trees in the forest. Amazingly, after the most devastating hurricanes, these trees would still be standing as if unscathed by the brute force of the winds, while almost every other tree would have succumbed to the battering. Now it doesn't take a rocket scientist to know that naturally, the tallest trees would be the ones to bear the brunt of the hurricane and be the first to fall; but not so with the tabonuco. What researchers found out was that the roots of these particular trees search underground once they begin to grow. Whenever it comes in contact with other trees of its kind, the roots intertwine and become as one. When it comes in contact with the roots of other trees, it just passes around them. The roots will only become one with other roots that are like it. The result is that every tabonuco tree within the forest, no matter how far they are from each other, forms a network underground which offers protection from the devastations above ground. When the powerful gusts would cause one to fall, the strength of the others would pull it back into place. That's how agreement works. It creates a united force which networks us so that whatever ill wind comes against one, the strength of the others would hold that one in place. The key thing is knowing that our strength alone cannot suffice but also knowing equally that we must exercise the greatest care in choosing who we come into agreement with.

There are two very destructive elements that the church grapples with today. One is the visionary who mistakenly believes that just because the vision is his, he can go it alone; that his anointing, his gifts, his ability are enough to bring it to fruition. Rather than finding, connecting and coming into agreement with gifted, faith driven people, he tries in his own strength to drive the vision along like a jockey whipping his mount to cross the finish line, prostituting the gifts, talents and abilities of others along the way to serve his own selfish ambitions. These are the churches which often start off with a bang but after a while the bang dies down and all that's left are him, his family and a faithful few who are only there because they have nowhere else to go. We are instructed by God through Habakkuk to write the vision and make it plain so that the ones who read it can run with it... catch the vision, come into agreement with it, embrace it and expend their time, effort, energy and ability into its success.

The other destructive element is the visionary who does not take care to choose who he brings into the vision with him, drafting individuals into the service based on title, degree, previous accomplishments and social standing, giving no regard for faith, faithfulness, commitment and those things which take precedence in Kingdom business. These are the churches which are never free of schisms and internal warfare because they have come into agreement with persons who do not really agree with them or have no heart for the vision, rather, just seeking to make a name for themselves.

In Acts chapter twelve we see how agreement among the people of God refuted the purposes of the strong opposition of Herod and the Jews who sought their demise. James was put to death by Herod who was ruler over that region and the death of James pleased the Jews. Ever wonder why some attacks come up against you sometimes, for no obvious reason? The glory on your life, the anointing you carry within and the light you emanate disturbs the opposition. Your presence makes many folks around you uncomfortable.

And rather than getting in line and coming in agreement with the glory of God on your life, they would rather fight against it in an attempt to suppress it. Much of the oppression you face is the enemy's attempt to suppress you.

When Herod saw that the death of James pleased the Jews, he proceeded to kill Peter also but because of Jewish custom, he could not be put to death at that particular time so he was placed in lockup within the inner prison with four quarternions of soldiers assigned to guard him. Four quarternions... that's sixteen soldiers in all working on shifts in groups of four, changing shift every four hours or so. Peter was chained between two of the soldiers and the other two guarded the door. Now, why in the world would you need such a high level of security for a simple preacher? This was not a reputed drug lord or an infamous mob boss. He was just a preacher for crying out loud! Well, maybe not. What Herod and the Jews knew from experience, and what we know now beyond a shadow of a doubt is that when you're an ambassador for Christ, there's nothing simple about you. There are forces that fight for you which are not of this world. Vain is the attempt of your opposition to employ earthly means to oppose you.

For the duration of Peter's incarceration, the church was in agreement, praying for his deliverance.

> *Acts 12:5*
> *Peter therefore was kept in prison: but prayer was made without ceasing of the church unto God for him.*

What blew my mind from this passage was Peter's attitude in the crisis. In just a matter of hours he was to be put to death and Peter was sleeping!

> *Acts 12:6*
> *And when Herod would have brought him forth, the same night Peter was sleeping between two soldiers, bound with two chains: and the keepers before the door kept the prison.*

Is this for real? How could he sleep at a time like this? Death was waiting for him on the other side of the night and the man was sleeping! Think about the simple things that cause us to lose rest night after night. We don't know where the money is coming from to pay our electricity bill; didn't get the promotion we were looking towards; bank loan payment overdue and the funds are short; landlord coming tomorrow and we don't have the funds yet. When compared to what Peter faced, these are light matters, and yet, not only was he asleep, but he made himself comfortable. When the angel of his deliverance came into the prison, he smote Peter on his side to wake him up and then instructed him to put on his belt, his shoes and his coat. Inside the inner prison, one can imagine, must have been hot.

Peter rested in comfort. As the Angel instructed Peter, the chains fell off of its own will; the doors opened of their own accord and Peter found himself standing in the streets. All this time the soldiers were still watching, completely oblivious to what was taking place. As far as they were concerned, Peter was still there in chains in the cell. Now, some people apply the reasoning that the soldiers were asleep and that explains why they were not aware of the prison break. I beg to differ. Firstly, the scriptures give no argument in support of that and secondly, remember that the soldiers worked on shifts for approximately four hours per shift. This was practically a fresh set of soldiers who had no need for sleep. This was the miraculous might of God at work.

So mind blowing was the deliverance that Peter himself never knew it was real until he found himself standing in the streets. All the while he thought he was dreaming. There is no limit to what God is willing and able to do when He finds those on earth who are willing to come into agreement to let His kingdom come and His will be done in earth as it is in Heaven. Upon realising that this thing was for real, the first thing Peter did was to go to the place where the church gathered in agreement on his behalf.

> *Acts 12:12*
> *And when he had considered the thing, he came to the house of Mary the mother of John, whose surname was Mark; where many were gathered together praying.*

So swift and awesome was the work of God that even those who stood in agreement were in disbelief at first. Notice what Peter did? He could have fled the country immediately in search of safe haven from Herod. Instead, he went first to the place where the church was agreeing in prayer on his behalf. He presented himself to them as living testimony that what they were agreeing for was done. We have to make it a habit to encircle ourselves with those who are in agreement with the vision and calling on our lives rather than surrounding ourselves with the mercenaries of the enemy who serve no other purpose than to slaughter our dreams and visions before they even get off the ground.

That wasn't the end of the script. God is not one to leave a story unfinished. He which has begun a thing will bring it to completion, we can rest assured in that. It was now daybreak. The day for Herod to seal his favour with the Jews by putting his prisoner to death, but when he sent for him, Peter was not there. The empty cell was there, the soldiers were there, the chains were there but Peter had escaped!

> *Acts 12:18-19*
> *18 Now as soon as it was day, there was no small stir among the soldiers, what was become of Peter.*
> *19 And when Herod had sought for him, and found him not, he examined the keepers, and commanded that they should be put to death. And he went down from Judaea to Caesarea, and there abode.*

Herod was so infuriated because of the premature end to his diabolic desire that he commanded the warders to be put to death. Someone had to take the fall for this. Get ready for a switch, the table is turning. Whatever was meant to work against you is turning in your favour and the evil that was determined is about to manifest upon the very ones who sold themselves as instruments of evil against you. And God will not stop until the transaction is complete. Look what happened to Herod.

> *Acts 12:23-24*
> *23 And immediately the angel of the Lord smote him, because he gave not God the glory: and he was eaten of worms, and gave up the ghost.*
> *24 But the word of God grew and multiplied.*

Out of pride and arrogance he sought to slaughter the people of God and that same pride and arrogance led to his own awful demise. But the word of the God grew and multiplied. All Herod's efforts to stifle the preaching and teaching of the Gospel and thereby abort the advancement of the Kingdom of God, only served to fertilise the work of the Kingdom. He failed to realise that none can stand against God and prevail. The greatest opposition will only work out for God's glory and to the advantage of the citizens of His Kingdom.

I come in agreement with you right now child of God, in the name of Jesus. I declare by faith that the mind blowing, saving power of Almighty God shall work swiftly and with precision on your behalf. Every opposition that has risen up against you shall be confounded. Every prison bar set up round about you shall open before you of its own accord in the name of Jesus. Prison bars of failure, lack, depression, poverty, stress, hurts, sicknesses, burdens, negative cycles and recurrent problems shall open now. Every chain used to shackle you in an uncomfortable and undesirable situation shall fall off now in Jesus' name. I agree with you through Christ that you are stepping out of obscurity. Limitations and restrictions will have no further effect on you. Your Heavenly Father bears you up on eagle's wings, therefore, you soar above obstacles, barriers and hindrances that were meant to stop your progress. In the name of Jesus, we two agree on earth that you are stepping into a new realm; a higher dimension. Your past will not follow you into your future. That which the Lord has ordained for your life shall be your portion. This is a new season. It's the season of double; the season of divine release. We agree together that you are blessed in Jesus' name. Amen!

Agreement on earth creates a
harmony that stirs Heaven to respond in
your favour.

Conditioning Your Condition

CONDITIONING YOUR CONDITION

"Don't allow your conditions to condition you; you must condition your condition." This is by far, one of the greatest pearls of wisdom that has ever bejewelled my life on this earth. You can never allow the struggles, hardships and negative occurrences that you face in life dictate how you live. You can never allow them to determine your level of happiness and contentment. You are greater than your present condition. You are not what you go through. Your situation is not your identification. Those circumstances are not your social security number or tax registration number as we use in Jamaica. Yes, God will allow them to work in some way for your good and for His glory, but you are not what you go through. You are greater.

My mind settles on the three Hebrew boys. Shadrach, Meshach and Abednego defied the Babylonian king's command and refused to bow down to the golden image which he erected. We find the account of this in Daniel chapter three. A brief synopsis of their lives is found in the first chapter of the book. These Hebrews were royalties in their homeland, then their condition changed. They were taken captive and brought to Babylon to serve the king. One of the things we need to understand about the nature of negative conditions is that they try to get you to look like them. Upon being taken to Babylon, these Hebrew royals had their names changed; each given name reflected Babylonian custom or paid homage to the Babylonian gods. After erecting the image, the command was issued that at the sound of the music, every person, regardless of race or creed, was to bow down and worship the image. The Hebrews were resolute in their stance. No other God except Jehovah, the True and Living God, would receive their worship. Nebuchadnezzar, upon beholding the unshakeable mindset of these men, burned with such anger that he commanded that the servants of God be cast into a furnace that was prepared and heated seven times hotter than necessary. But even in the midst of the fire, God was with them. The condition (the fire) that was prepared for them could do them no harm. Look at the result:

> *Daniel 3:24-27*
> *24 Then Nebuchadnezzar the king was astonied, and rose up in haste, and spake, and said unto his counsellors, Did not we cast three men bound into the midst of the fire? They answered and said unto the king, True, O king.*
> *25 He answered and said, Lo, I see four men loose, walking in the midst of the fire, and they have no*

hurt; and the form of the fourth is like the Son of God.

26 Then Nebuchadnezzar came near to the mouth of the burning fiery furnace, and spake, and said, Shadrach, Meshach, and Abednego, ye servants of the most high God, come forth, and come hither. Then Shadrach, Meshach, and Abednego, came forth of the midst of the fire.

27 And the princes, governors, and captains, and the king's counsellors, being gathered together, saw these men, upon whose bodies the fire had no power, nor was an hair of their head singed, neither were their coats changed, nor the smell of fire had passed on them.

They were not scorched, their clothes were intact, their hairs were not singed and they did not even smell of smoke. They came out of the condition without looking or smelling like the condition because they did not allow the condition to condition them; they conditioned their condition. They were living testimonies of what God promised through the prophet Isaiah:

Isaiah 43:2
When thou passest through the waters, I will be with thee; and through the rivers, they shall not overflow thee: when thou walkest through the fire, thou shalt not be burned; neither shall the flame kindle upon thee.

Every single human on the face of the earth is faced with his or her own struggle. It may be in the form of rejection, depression, fear, low self-esteem, constant lack, persistent failure, lingering sickness, a troubled marriage, unstable family life. Whatever label is on the package, everyone deals with a struggle. There are seasons in which some of us are plagued with a flurry of negative situations, one behind the other or sometimes coming all at once. These struggles - these negative conditions, are battling against our peace of mind to gain the advantage to reprogram our mindset and put us in a state where we accept the life that it dictates. It is not only evident with humans but also seen throughout nature. It was reported that scientists conducted a series of experiments which they call behavioural conditioning. In one such experiment, a dog, which by nature is aggressive, was chained. At feeding time, its food was placed just beyond the reach of the chain. The vicious, hungry animal made one lunge toward the meal, only to be yanked back by the chain. The scientists continued this procedure for about three days. The next day, the chain was removed and the food was placed in the same position. Rather than lunging toward the meal, the beast laid still without moving. What happened? Its mind was conditioned to believe that if he moved, the result would be the same as it was for the past three days. Its mindset was so subdued that it could not even realise that it was no longer restricted by the fetters. This is exactly what happens with many of us. Some conditions are so persistent that we lose the will to fight; to persevere, and we slump into a state of accepting what the condition presents to us.

If we are to be conditioners of our conditions rather than being conditioned by them, there has to be a reprogramming of our minds. Paul addresses this same issue:

> *Romans 12:2*
> *And be not conformed to this world: but be ye transformed by the renewing of your mind, that ye may prove what is that good, and acceptable, and perfect, will of God.*

The word "conform" from its Greek origin is "syschēmatízō" which means to fashion one's self according to someone else's pattern. "Transform" in Greek is "metamorphóō" from which we derive the word "metamorphosis". Translated to English, it means to change into another form. What was he trying to get across to us? Do not assume or take on someone else's pattern or allow any outer factor, force or condition to determine how your life is fashioned, rather, change into another form completely different from what your present conditions dictate. In other words, be like the caterpillar... an unsightly creature that is scorned by many. It's hard to imagine that it can be anything but a destructive insect crawling around in search of the next plant to devour. But encoded into the DNA of the uncomely crawler is the power of transformation not conformation. It changes form, regardless of what people think about it; regardless of its limitations, it becomes a butterfly. It does not allow the condition of our scornful attitude towards it to prevent it from fulfilling its destiny - it changes. And so drastic is the change that it cannot go back to what it was before.

Okay then, we hear what you're saying Brother Paul. We must transform and not conform. But just how are we to accomplish that? Well, he explains how. It's by the renewing of our minds. The word "renew" comes from the Greek "anakaínōsis" which means to renew; renovate; make a complete change for the better. Note well, that the apostle did not implore us to recycle our minds. If that were the case, we would still possess the same mindset in a new package. He instead implored us to renovate our minds: make a complete change for the better; get rid of the old, worn out, dilapidated mental furniture and appliances that crowd our minds and replace them with the new spiritual upgrades from the Kingdom of God. Renew your mind through the Word of God. Where you were conditioned to accept defeat, declare that you are more than a conqueror. Where you were conditioned to accept failure, declare that God makes your way prosperous and gives you good success. Where you were conditioned to accept poverty, declare that God has given you power to get wealth. Where you were conditioned to accept sickness, declare that with His stripes you are healed. Whatever the conditions that seek to condition you, turn the tables on them through the Word of the Living God.

Alright, time for an experiment. Let's get into the mental laboratory and do a theoretic practical, if there's such a thing. Imagine that you have before you, a stove and three containers of water. In addition, you have a carrot, an egg and a tea bag. Ok now, light the burners and bring the containers of water to a boil. Upon boiling, place each item in the containers and observe the outcome. What happens to the carrot as it boils? The state of it changes. It was hard and crunchy but the hot water causes it to lose its crunchiness. It becomes soft. What happens to the egg? Its state also changes. It was fragile and the substance was of a liquid nature. The hot water has causes it to become hard. Final item: the tea bag. What are your observations? The tea bag has changed the state of the water. As a matter of fact, it's no longer water. It has become tea.

You see, the hot water represents the condition. There are some folks who are like the carrot. Whenever they face certain conditions, the conditions change their state. They become soft, easily hurt, fearful, worrisome, depressed. They lose their sense of self-worth. There are those who, after facing certain conditions, become hard just like the egg. They become cold and callous, without compassion or affection. Then there are those who refuse to allow the conditions to affect them, instead, they use what is in them to affect the condition. They are like the tea bag. May we all develop that resolve, that no matter what we go through, the circumstances will not cause us to become soft, weak and defeated. Nor will they cause us to become hard and callous. Rather, we will add flavour to our circumstances. They will not dictate our living; we dictate their operations.   Jesus gave us a perfect demonstration of this:

> *Mark 11:12-14 & 19-23*
> *12 And on the morrow, when they were come from Bethany, he was hungry:*
> *13 And seeing a fig tree afar off having leaves, he came, if haply he might find any thing thereon: and when he came to it, he found nothing but leaves; for the time of figs was not yet.*
> *14 And Jesus answered and said unto it, No man eat fruit of thee hereafter for ever. And his disciples heard it.*
> *19 And when even was come, he went out of the city.*
> *20 And in the morning, as they passed by, they saw the fig tree dried up from the roots.*
> *21 And Peter calling to remembrance saith unto him, Master, behold, the fig tree which thou cursedst is withered away.*
> *22 And Jesus answering saith unto them, Have faith in God.*

> *23 For verily I say unto you, That whosoever shall say unto this mountain, Be thou removed, and be thou cast into the sea; and shall not doubt in his heart, but shall believe that those things which he saith shall come to pass; he shall have whatsoever he saith.*

As Jesus and His disciples went on their journey, a condition presented itself to Him; He became hungry. It was not the time of year for fig trees to produce but as Jesus looked in the distance He saw a fig tree which He hoped would at least have something on it for Him to satisfy His hunger. As He came and examined the branches, He found that all this tree had to offer were leaves. Now the first thing that explodes in this passage is what takes place in verse fourteen. It says "and Jesus answered and said unto it..." Jesus answered the tree. Just hold up one minute. To answer someone or something means to respond to something that was said before. As a matter of fact, the Greek word used is "apokrínomai" meaning, to begin to speak but always where something has preceded (either said or done) to which the remarks refer. Now, if Jesus answered the fig tree, then it stands to reason that the fig tree was speaking to Him in the first place. What could it possibly have been saying? "Jesus, you're hungry and you'll die of hunger". Whatever conditions we face, we must understand that those conditions are constantly speaking, making negative reinforcements in our minds and over our lives. We must therefore learn how to respond to our conditions.

What did Jesus say? "Never again will anyone eat any fruit from you", and He ensured that His disciples heard it because this for them was a valuable lesson. As they were passing by in just a matter of hours, heading back in the opposite direction, they noticed that the tree was withered. The very same fig tree that Jesus spoke to just a few hours before was dead, dried up from the roots. A process which should have taken months if not years, was done in just a matter of hours at the command of Jesus. Peter expressed marvel at the sight but Jesus calmly replied "have faith in God." The key to conditioning your conditions is not just to rehearse scripture but to speak the Word of God by faith. Follow carefully the instruction of Jesus: "say - do not doubt - believe". That's faith! He says whosoever applies this principle, anyone who uses this key, whatever is said shall come to pass.

I met a young woman a number of years ago. It was during an all-night prayer vigil. It was the first time I was laying eyes on her but what drew me was the anointing that flowed as she led the worship. Cutting a long story short, we got engaged some time later. At that time, I was employed to an institution in a temporary capacity and my tenure had just come to an end. The wedding date was set for approximately seven months down the road and I was exercising crazy, mountain top faith that another job was going to open up in time, and it did - two months before the wedding date. It was at a multi-grade school in which classes were paired together. I was employed as a pre-trained teacher to teach grades seven, eight and nine which were grouped together in one class. For the first month I received no salary because my documents were not submitted to the Ministry of Education in time. After a few weeks on the job, the principal, who also doubled as the teacher for grades five and six, fell ill. And guess what? I was now the teacher of grades five, six, seven, eight and nine; me - a pre-trained teacher. After two months of work, just a short time before the wedding, my salary finally came through. When I went to collect it, I was presented with another envelop. In it was a letter which stated that my work performance was not satisfactory and therefore they have no choice but to let me go. I was like "what! Let me go! After the injustice of burying me head first under five grades when there were others there who were trained and more qualified to handle those responsibilities than I was!" But all glory to God! the pay checks that I received, (the one for the previous month which was delayed and the one for the current month), provided us with enough funds to cover wedding expenses.

We got married at the end of July and by August I was back at it again, hunting for a job. The condition was speaking to us... "you'll never be able to pay your rent; they're gonna cut off your electricity; your water supply will be disconnected." Despite all this, we held on to the principle of speaking life and calling those things which were not as though they were. We were conditioning the condition. I was invited to a particular church to preach one Sunday. At the end of the service I was informed of two positions that had opened up in a preparatory school in the area. I submitted my application for both positions, hoping that I would find favour with one of them. On the day of the interview my heart sank when I saw the massive crowd of aspirants that had gathered. What made it worse was that I knew the level of experience and qualification that some of them possessed. There was that taunting little voice prodding me to just throw in the towel, save myself the embarrassment and leave, there's no way I could get in with those folks in line. My name was called. I entered the room. The chairman of the school board, the principal and another member of the board were there. I sat facing them and the chairman began the questioning. Suddenly, he was interrupted by the principal. She was a member of the church where I was invited to preach a few days before and she was sitting in the congregation as I ministered. She began speaking on my behalf, persuading the board members to hire me for one of the positions. Fast forward... I got the job but it was just for four months. At the end of my tenure, the principal and senior teacher spoke to the board once again on my behalf which resulted in them creating a position in the institution for me; a position which I occupied for eleven years. I resigned from that job a few years ago of my own free will. Why was all this possible? Because we applied the principle of conditioning our conditions by speaking the word of faith and not allowing the condition to impose its terms on our living.

Sometimes all we can do in some situations is stand in faith and speak the Word until we see the desired change. There are other situations in which speaking the word is just not enough. There has to be a practical application of faith in order for the condition to be conditioned; that kind of "Peter posture" where we climb over the side of the boat and begin to walk on the very thing that wanted to walk over us. That kind of attitude where we become so righteously violent that we step out in fearless confidence, letting the storm know that "enough is enough. I don't care how big the waves are that you stir up against me. I may have been designed to walk on land and not on water, but just so you know that greater is He that is in me than whatever force it is that drives you, I'm gonna walk on you anyway". Sometimes you have to wake up the David in you when Goliath has already sapped the courage of everyone else around you, conditioning them with fear and dismay to the point where they have already embraced defeat. Every time you try to move forward with your vision here comes another whimpering warrior telling you that it doesn't make sense, it won't work, you'll only fail because they've already tried it and it can't be done. You see, Goliath's aim is for the people of God lose heart, lose hope and become weak in their faith in God. Face that Goliath of a condition head on. Declare to it that it's not by your might or power but by the Spirit of God and in the name of the Lord that you stand. Put a stone of faith in the sling of your mouth, hurl it into the forehead of that ghastly beat, knock it into submission and use the sword of the Spirit which is the Word of God to decapitate it. When it loses its head, it loses its authority and its ability to exercise influence over you.

One of the most powerful Biblical examples of conditioning your condition through practical faith is the story of four unnamed men in the Old Testament. The only information we are provided with as to their identity is that they were lepers. It was during the time when Benhadad and the Syrian host besieged Samaria and stirred up one of the greatest recessions ever recorded. So sore was the condition upon the land that the most undesirable meal servings were way above the pay grade of many Samaritans. Women even resorted to boiling and eating their children.

2 Kings 6:24-29
24 And it came to pass after this, that Benhadad king of Syria gathered all his host, and went up, and besieged Samaria.
25 And there was a great famine in Samaria: and, behold, they besieged it, until an ass's head was sold for fourscore pieces of silver, and the fourth part of a cab of dove's dung for five pieces of silver.
26 And as the king of Israel was passing by upon the wall, there cried a woman unto him, saying, Help, my lord, O king.
27 And he said, If the LORD do not help thee, whence shall I help thee? out of the barnfloor, or out of the winepress?
28 And the king said unto her, What aileth thee? And she answered, This woman said unto me, Give thy son, that we may eat him to day, and we will eat my son to morrow.
29 So we boiled my son, and did eat him: and I said unto her on the next day, Give thy son, that we may eat him: and she hath hid her son.

Now according to ceremonial law, anyone suffering from leprosy was to remain outside the city until he either recovered or was pronounced dead. Family and friends must have considered these leprous men long dead given the severity of the famine and the intensity of the suffering that it brought on. The disease was already eating away at them, there's no way they could survive the onslaught of hunger that the city was dealing with. But there's one thing the people of God can rest assured in: anything God allows, there's always a greater purpose being worked out than what the eyes can see and when that purpose works out, it will always bring Him glory. Samaria was besieged, famine was raging but God was about to show forth His glory and the awesomeness of His might through four nameless, forgotten men.

The scriptures do say that anything God does, He first makes it known through His servants, the prophets.

> *Amos 3:7*
> *Surely the Lord GOD will do nothing, but he revealeth his secret unto his servants the prophets.*

The Lord spoke through Elisha, revealing to the king of Israel and his advisors, what was about to happen. Now, whenever God speaks, it would do us well to run with it and even if it seems impossible to the extent that we become doubtful, it would be best to be silent and reserve any expression of doubt. God is not limited or restricted to the timing, ability or mindset of men. He saves and delivers in ways that only He can. When He moves, the manifestations of His glory are undeniable, cannot be refuted and cannot be attributed to anyone else. God told Elisha to tell the people that recession was going to end in twenty four hours, inflation was going to be turned around and as a matter of fact, they were not going to have enough, they were going to have more than enough! To those looking through the eyes of the condition, this was an impossible thing. It's just not possible to leave from eating our children one day and go into a buffet style feast the next! Such was the attitude of one of the king's most trusted advisors. Hear his words:

> *2 Kings 7:2*
> *Then a lord on whose hand the king leaned answered the man of God, and said, Behold, if the LORD would make windows in heaven, might this thing be? And he said, Behold, thou shalt see it with thine eyes, but shalt not eat thereof.*

Notice the response of the prophet: "you shall see it but you shall not taste it." The very same doubtful advisor was trampled to death in a stampede for food within twenty four hours just as the Lord had spoken through the mouth of Elisha. Never look at your condition through the eyes of the condition or you will never see beyond the condition itself. When you look through the eyes of faith, the most gargantuan condition becomes minuscule and insignificant. But just how did God cause the prophetic word of Elisha to come to pass? The four leprous men began having a faith conversation among themselves. They began to examine the nature and extremity of their condition.

2 Kings 7:3-4

3 And there were four leprous men at the entering in of the gate: and they said one to another, Why sit we here until we die?

4 If we say, We will enter into the city, then the famine is in the city, and we shall die there: and if we sit still here, we die also. Now therefore come, and let us fall unto the host of the Syrians: if they save us alive, we shall live; and if they kill us, we shall but die.

Their conclusion was that the city holds no hope. They are in no better position than we are. If we go there it's certain death. If we stay here, death is also guaranteed. What lesson does this reasoning hold for us? People who are praying, hoping and expecting change, should not surround themselves with people who will only hold them in the said state they are desperate to escape from. Neither is it acceptable to sit and expect change to fall in your lap. You have to move by faith but also be guided by wisdom. They decided to venture into the camp of the very people who were holding them hostage. That was the only place where hope was and there was the possibility that they might spare their lives. Stepping out in faith opens the door for you to find favour in unfavourable places.

The fragrance of their faith attracted God. These men, who were cloaked in sores, scorned and deemed unworthy to be around their own people, attracted the attention of the King of Kings. Remember what is said concerning faith in the book of Hebrews?

> *Hebrews 11:6*
> *But without faith it is impossible to please him: for he that cometh to God must believe that he is, and that he is a rewarder of them that diligently seek him.*

Faith pleases God. The lepers made their faith move. It was now God's turn. Now remember, these men were covered with sores from the crowns of their heads to the soles of their feet as the nature of leprosy is. They could not walk as ordinary, healthy men. Their steps were tender and one can imagine, with some degree of pain. It was perhaps almost impossible to hear the sound of their feet as they slowly progressed toward the Syrian base. But God, in His awesome might, amplified and magnified the stealthy steps of four men, just eight leprous feet, to sound like the armies of two of the greatest fighting forces in the world at that time combined.

> *2 Kings 7:6-7*
> *6 For the Lord had made the host of the Syrians to hear a noise of chariots, and a noise of horses, even the noise of a great host: and they said one to another, Lo, the king of Israel hath hired against us the kings of the Hittites, and the kings of the Egyptians, to come upon us.*

> *7 Wherefore they arose and fled in the twilight, and left their tents, and their horses, and their asses, even the camp as it was, and fled for their life.*

Needless to say, the end result was in favour of the people of God. The Syrians fled at the overwhelming noise of the massive army of four leprous men marching toward them. This was God's move... Checkmate! Through four nameless, forgotten men who activated faith to condition their condition, the condition of the entire city was transformed in twenty four hours.

Whatever condition it is that opposes you right now, activate faith, attract the presence of the Almighty and watch him break forth upon the condition like the floods of many waters. I declare that victory is yours. Triumph is within your grasp. You shall yet praise God. Your present condition is not your final resting place in the name of Jesus. DON'T ALLOW YOUR CONDITION TO CONDITION YOU... YOU MUST CONDITION YOUR CONDITION!

Condition Your Condition

Just as the tea bag changes the hot water that it is placed in, you have the power within you to change every condition you are faced with. Don't let your conditions condition you… you must condition your condition.

Poetic

Declaration

POETIC DECLARATION

Father I exalt You,
You are the King of Kings of Kings,
Sovereign over the universe
And over all created things.
By the word of your mouth
All life is held in place,
And daily I'm renewed
By Your amazing grace.

I'm cleansed by Jesus' blood,
My life is free from all stains,
And the same blood that cleansed me
Now flows through my veins.
The accuser of the brethren
Has no evidence on me,
Christ has advocated
And the King has set me free.

It's on now devil,
you've messed with the wrong one,
Didn't your demons tell you
That I'm God's anointed son?
By the blood I rebuke and rout you
And all your hellish host
I discomfit you by the power
Of the Holy Ghost.

Everything you have stolen
I take it back by force;
My conditions will not condition me
Because the Lord directs my course.
There's a wall of fire around me,
You can't access where I abide,
and every demon you unleash
Will only fall down at my side.

Purpose is within me,
I carry precious cargo on board,
In my heart there's a flaming fire,
In my mouth there's a two-edged sword,
I speak life to the life I'm living
And death to the death you've planned
I am more than a conqueror
Through Jehovah in whom I stand.

I'm before and not behind,
I'm the head and not the tail;
My enemies must be blind,
Can't they see they'll only fail?
My King has crowned me with glory,
He has abundantly blessed my days;
Christ is the Author of my story,
There's a Lion in my praise!

ABOUT KABOWD MINISTRIES

But we all, with open face, beholding... the glory of the Lord, are changed into the same image from glory to glory, even as by the Spirit of the Lord.
2 Corinthians 3: 18 (KJV)

Kabowd Ministries was founded by Elon and Stacey Talmie by inspiration of God through the Holy Spirit (*But there is a spirit in man, the inspiration of the Almighty giveth him understanding. Job 32:8 KJV*). The ministry was birthed out of a passion to fulfill the will, purpose and intent of God for their lives and to see others embracing their God-ordained purpose.

The word 'Kabowd' is of Hebrew origin and is found throughout the Old Testament. When translated to English it means 'glory' and refers to the majesty, splendour, might and heaviness of God.

OUR VISION

Kabowd Ministries is established with the purpose of impacting the spirit, soul and body of man by manifesting and advancing the Kingdom of God in the earth, allowing His Kingdom to come and His will to be done just as it is in Heaven.

OUR MISSION

This ministry exists to be an avenue of salvation, transformation, healing and deliverance through the ministering of the full gospel of the Kingdom of God, guiding individuals to their purpose in the name of Jesus Christ the Son of God, by the power of the Holy Spirit the Governor of the Kingdom, to the glory of God the Father – The King of Kings of Kings.

THE DIRECTORS

Elon Talmie was born on September 9, 1980. Stacey Talmie, nee Campbell, was born on September 10, 1980. By divine design, their paths crossed twenty years later during an all-night prayer vigil and on July 20, 2002, the two became one flesh. Through them, the vision for Kabowd Ministries was birthed.

Elon is a teacher of the Word of God. His spiritual journey began in the Church of God of Prophecy. After a short period in the United Church in Jamaica and the Cayman Islands he transitioned into the position of youth pastor of a non-denominational ministry where his wife also served as worship leader and director of children's ministry. Elon brings to light, the revelations of the Gospel of the Kingdom and places emphasis on purpose. He is a motivational/inspirational speaker and addresses audiences in church/spiritual events, family and community events and school based events.

Stacey, before becoming a part of the United Church with her husband, was a member of the New Testament Church of God. She is an anointed psalmist, worshipper and songwriter and is gifted to work with children both on a spiritual and educational level.

Together, they minister across various denominations on an itinerant basis with an aim to spur spiritual growth and advancement, fulfilling the call to be ambassadors for Christ.